THE ENTREPRENEUR WITHIN YOU
VOLUME 3

THE ENTREPRENEUR WITHIN YOU
VOLUME 3

Curated BY

Julie M. Holloway

Graphic design by Julie M. Holloway
www.jmhcre8ive.com

Edited by Tiff's Editing Café

ISBN: 978-1514879214

Printed in the United States

Welcome

As you make your way through the TEW journey, we invite you to interact with us on social media using the hashtags #unleashthebiz and #TEW3

Twitter @ TEWYou
Facebook @ TheEntrepreneurWithinYou

Be.Inspired!

TABLE OF CONTENTS

Foreword by Monique Caradine - 15
1. What's My Why? – Julie M. Holloway - 21
2. Create and Inspire to Enable Others to See They Can Create – Josh Renner - 25
3. God's Plan Is Always Better Than Your Plan! – Andrea "Dre" Nichols Everett - 33
4. To Have and to Hold, from this Business Forward – Carrie Elaine Forman - 55
5. Build your BRAND, start a LEGACY! – Vau've A. Davis - 63
6. From The Chaos of a Startup to the Calm from a Profit – Pierre DeBois - 73
7. Tips for Elevating, Success, Inspiration, Growth + Pushing Through – Tamika Maria Price - 85
8. Out Living the Circumstances – Renee Jefferson Smith - 93
9. Delayed is not Denied – LaTasha West - 101
10. The Birth of Windy City Mix – Rodrigo Alvear - 107
11. Learn How to Succeed in Any Circumstance – Dr. Toi Dennis – 119
12. Love All and Happiness – Kasia Wereszczynska , M.A., LCPC, RYT - 127
13. The Power (and Profit) in Partnership – Summer Alexander and Laura E. Knights, LCSW "The Savvy Solopreneurs" - 135
14. Starting and Running My Businesses – Daniel C. Lewis - 149
15. To Begin ~ you must begin – Marti Hannon - 155
16. The Truth About Entrepreneurship – Angelia Hopson - 163

17. Stand for Something, it's Your Business Brand! – Rai Barney - 181
18. The Process of Success – Tonya Biglow - 187
19. Anything is possible! – Ocie Duncan IV - 195
20. First Things First – Tiffany M. Stevens - 201
21. Why What I Do Matters... – C. Lynn Williams, Ms. Parent Guru - 209

TEW Journal by Diane Brown - 217

DEDICATION

TEW is dedicated to entrepreneurs trying, doing, risking, attempting, creating and simply making great things happen. It is also dedicated to our families who so passionately support us.

TEW THE MOVEMENT

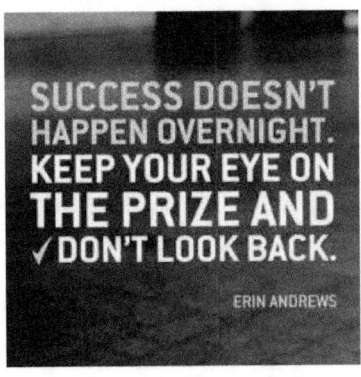

SUCCESS DOESN'T HAPPEN OVERNIGHT. KEEP YOUR EYE ON THE PRIZE AND ✓ DON'T LOOK BACK.

ERIN ANDREWS

• • •

The Entrepreneur Within You is an inspirational business anthology series that consists of a collection of experiences from a diverse group of entrepreneurs. The authors of the book not only share with the readers how their path to business ownership began; they also include encouraging personal stories of challenges conquered, along with tips and tools that aspiring entrepreneurs can use to accomplish their goals, despite facing their own version of these very same obstacles.

The experiences that our writers share will motivate all who are moved to turn its pages! We are fulfilling our destiny by allowing real entrepreneurs a platform to share their trials and then their triumphs, ultimately passing on the torch of dreams held by many savvy and successful entrepreneurs.

FOREWORD

Monique Caradine

Success does not have like to be strangled in the hands of desperation. It needs time to spread it's wings and become what it is meant to be. - Beverly Garb

• • •

I knew there was an entrepreneur within me back in the mid 1990s. My husband and I were dating then and he had decided to start his own business. We were fresh out of college. I was working as an administrative assistant at a boutique public relations firm and he had just finished his first year working at what was then one of the top technology companies in the world. Even though his future there was bright, he knew he did not want to work a job forever.

So his entrepreneurial pursuit began. About once a week after work, we would go to our local OfficeMax to get the supplies he needed to get his home office up and running—file folders, a printer, paper clips, business cards, sticky notes, etc.

After a while, going to OfficeMax became a highlight in my day. I would get giddy as I roamed the isles. It was just amazing to know that if I ever decided to start a business, all the tools I needed were right in this store. I didn't know what kind of business it would be but for me this store represented endless possibilities. I was literally getting "high" on office supply!

That's how I knew I would start my own business one day. Yes, it sounds weird but this is a peek at what goes on in the mind of the entrepreneur.

You see entrepreneurs are a very unique breed. Our interests are different. While some people get turned on by things like fashion or cars, we get turned on by the latest productivity tools and invoicing apps.

Our thinking patterns are also different. At any given moment, a burst of excitement will come through and suddenly our conversation is laced with an unmistakable zeal for our next big crazy idea.

We sleep differently, we hustle differently, we schedule our day differently and we process success and failure differently. We are unlike any other group of people, and because of that we are often completely misunderstood.

Can you relate?

That's why I am so glad that you found this book. By bringing together this diverse and dynamic group of game changers, Julie Holloway has done three things that are vitally important to the success of entrepreneurs. First, she has **created a community** of people who have endured the hard knocks of starting a business. By reading their stories you'll see the value in surrounding yourself with other entrepreneurs who have not only survived but thrived through the tough times.

You see, many new entrepreneurs make the mistake of thinking that their success is a solo effort but I can tell you for sure, it is not. We also make the deadly mistake of trying to explain entrepreneurial ideas to people who work 9-to-5 jobs for a living. Only do that if you want to kill the entrepreneur within you! You must have accountability from a success-oriented community of other entrepreneurs.

So leverage the brilliance and expertise you will find within these pages. Start a discussion group or a meet-up centered around this book so that other entrepreneurs can get together and support one another. If you are really bold, connect with some of the authors featured here and invite them to speak. Invest in their mentorship. Do whatever it takes to learn from them so you can avoid common pitfalls and begin to accelerate your success.

Secondly, this powerful compilation also gives you **instant access to people who have probably failed more times than they have succeeded** but they still refused to give up. You get to hear from people who have put everything on the line to bring their dream to life. In the process, some have lost money, friends and even family but they persevered because of that unstoppable, indescribable, often misunderstood internal vision that drives most entrepreneurs. Do you have that drive?

Lastly, this book gives you **proof that becoming an entrepreneur will cost you.** You will absolutely be required to put some skin in this game. Do you have a thin skin? Are your feelings easily hurt? If so, put this book down immediately and choose something else because you are not ready for this yet.

This brings me back to the story of my husband and me. He has now been in business for nearly 25 years. I watched him put in blood, sweat, tears and a lot of sleepless nights to grow his once solo-preneur technology company into a growing, multi-million dollar enterprise with more than a dozen employees. To this day, he is my greatest inspiration.

Meanwhile, I continued to roam through the aisles of my favorite office supply stores for a little while longer before I started my business. I just wasn't ready yet. I loved the idea of having my own business cards but the commitment and courage it took to actually be in business scared the shit out of me! So I happily worked for various radio and television stations for many years as an on-air personality.

Then, in 2003, I started Momentum Media Group. Even though my husband was my biggest supporter and we were a powerful community of two, I still made tons of mistakes, I failed frequently and I almost walked away from my business when the economy crashed in 2008.

Today however, I proudly wear my failures as a badge of honor because without them I wouldn't have the thriving business I have today. My business is now 11 years old and centered around my beautiful Caribbean lifestyle (we live full-time on the island of Puerto Rico). I haven't reached the million dollar mark yet but now that I am crystal-clear on the value that I bring to the marketplace, I am well on my way. More importantly though, I have the freedom and income to do the things I enjoy and I love the work I do as a success coach to some downright amazing women entrepreneurs. To me that is priceless!

Listen, entrepreneurship is not for wimps. People give up because it can be hard as hell. Sometimes the people closest to you will call you crazy. You will face rejection, defeat, doubt and fear. However, to succeed as an entrepreneur *your desire to bring your unique value to the marketplace has to be greater than your fear.*

So use this book as a guide to your success. Use it to gain courage. Use it to connect with your community. Not everyone is going to understand your hustle but the people in this book understand completely. Take it with you wherever you go. Read a chapter as you stand in line at the grocery store or sit under the dryer getting your hair done. Dog-ear the pages, highlight phrases and study, study, study. This book is now your bible for business. Let it equip and empower you to unleash your entrepreneur within.

I totally believe in you!

Monique Caradine
www.MoniqueCaradine.com

1

What's My WHY"?
Julie M. Holloway

"If the creative artist worries if he will still be free
tomorrow, then he will not be free today."
- Salman Rushdie

• • •

This year I set out to discover my "true" WHY. After much
artistic and internal exploration, I found these simple
words lit up my every day "let your soul sparkle."

I am Julie Holloway (best known as JMH). I am an artist,
author and graphic designer. For 16 years I worked in
corporate America only to realize I did not quite fit in.
My calling has always been my art and living a colorful
lifestyle. I can finally say that after 38 years on earth, I
am able to do that. I live and work from my home in
Hanover Park, IL with my husband Darnell and two
children, Jasmine and DJ (also budding authors and
very artistic).

A few years ago, I went through a tumultuous journey of
being slightly abused by my last boss. He was very
controlling, rude, argumentative and demanding. I
could not thrive while working for him no matter how

hard I tried. Out of the sheer need to voice my experiences of wanting so badly to be a full-time entrepreneur, to ultimately wanting to bless others with my "quit story," I began to write TEW. I want people to know that, "Dreams are REAL, and that sometimes, success is the best REVENGE for the ultimate challenge."

In TEW volume 1, I wrote quite a lengthy chapter. My focus was on wanting to quit, then about how I quit my job, and what happened 30/60/90 days after that. That chapter still gives me chills to this day, because as I recall it, I can feel the emotion, pain and passion deep within. I have a stinging inside that really propels me further each and every day now that I am working for myself. I knew as a child I wanted to be an artist. Drawing and painting were the ways I expressed myself, but I let them get away from me when needing to bring in money to support my family.

I went to The School of The Art Institute of Chicago for one year, quit, and never jumped into the art industry as a career. Everyone else was getting office jobs in the city, and I thought that was what I was supposed to do as well. Seven years ago this week I finally made the jump back into my passion for art and design. The company I was working for was going through a massive round of layoffs, and I knew I would be next. A cousin in Chicago asked me to design a logo, so I bought a program off of Craigslist for $50 and taught myself graphic design. I started freelancing, and my business grew from the ground up. I've now been able to include my other artistic talents, drawing and painting, into my design business.

When I became a full-time entrepreneur, I had zero balance and no one to keep me accountable. My husband Darnell was very supportive but didn't say anything as he wanted to give me space to allow me and my business to grow. I was like an entrepreneur zombie. Two years ago, my husband and I agreed that this needed to change. He worked with me to help me transition from a zombie to a healthier and happier business owner. Now, we have a habitual schedule. We eat all of our meals together, and I make sure to have specific times that are for family only. I still get burned out from time to time because being an entrepreneur is hard work, but I'm learning daily how to be better at what I do and I'm working to become an even better mother and wife.

After leaving a corporate job to start my business, I had to become a salesman, bill collector, accountant, financial planner, and marketer, when I really just wanted to focus on my artwork and graphic design. There just wasn't enough time to get everything done. At the end of each day, I felt like I had done everything except the actual work I had to deliver to clients. When dealing with all of the aspects of your business, it's hard to keep a creative mindset, which is a necessity for my work. It's gotten easier over time, but that was a major hurdle. It takes discipline and being able to give yourself the opportunity and time to relax and unwind. As entrepreneurs, we want to do it all, but sometimes that isn't possible.

I've been very lucky to have a lot of positive and influential mentors, friends and family members. My husband, mom, dad, and brother and sisters have been what have kept me going and their support keeps me positive and confident. My courage coach, Nicole Knox, has played an intricate part of my business for a few years now I've also had an influential high school art teacher, Mr. A. who has driven me to believe that I could become a professional artist, and dear friend Bernada Nicole Baker who has given me inspiration, encouragement and the answers that I've desperately needed at times. I'm very thankful, and I try to repay the support they've given me by creating a strong entrepreneurial community with The Entrepreneur Within You.

Aside from coffee, I need a strong network and the support of my family, which I've been lucky to have. The path of entrepreneurship is certainly not an easy one, and not straight-forward at all. You will learn lesson, after lesson, hardly knowing where you left off on the prior.

2

Create and Inspire to Enable Others to See They Can Create Leverage
Josh Renner

• • •

All things in this life are related in some way.
Have the faith push through.

I have always been business minded, ever since I was a teenager.

I started out by pulling weeds for a friend from my church, at his ranch. He was a building designer. In high school, I had taken drafting classes, so I had somewhat of the knowledge that was needed to draw like he did.

I was out in the yard, pulling weeds one day and he asked me if I could help him with something.

He was under a strict deadline on a project that he was working on and needed to also get another drawing completed at the same time.

So, he asked me if I could draw a set of complete plans for a garage. I said, "sure." It was then, the summer of my 18th year, that I started my design career.

That Fall, I started at San Diego State University and was planning on focusing on Architecture, since I was now drawing more and more small projects. It was then that my friend and new mentor was teaching me more and more about the business, how it worked and that I may want to become an entrepreneur under his design firm. I didn't even think that it was possible for an 18 year old kid to be an entrepreneur.

I was getting paid great for the design work that I was turning out. That meant that I would be my own business under his business's name. As time went by, I was learning more and more at work than I was in college. It was then that I decided to quit school and focus on my newly emerging business.

I was creating a VISION of my entire future self. Others around me thought that I was crazy and said that I would fail. As exciting as it was, there was a lot to learn about the various codes and ordinances that I would need to adhere to while designing my client's drawings.

My mentor even suggested that I start another inter-related business that has to do with Energy Conservation of the designs that we create. Very exciting to have TWO businesses that now were thriving.

Flash forward 25.5 years to where I am right now, as I am writing this. I am still here in the architecture and design industry, after suffering through 3 recessions, ups and downs in the market and learning so much about how the industry works. I was with my friend and mentor in his business, for just over 22 years. That was a long time. I am grateful for all that he taught me, guiding me towards how to run my businesses and make them grow and always taught me to put God first.

Since we are recently coming out of a very turbulent recession, I have seen many long standing colleagues around me close up shop and wither away. They had to do what they had to do to stay alive and pay their bills. And at the time, architecture was not going to provide that. People with disposable money is was the norm. People that could afford to build either room additions or brand new homes.

With the recession of 2008, that income from these types of people, literally disappeared over night. Where I was once pulling in six figures before the recession.......once it hit, I was losing projects, faster and faster. I was literally living below the poverty level, by the nation's definition. Talk about a scary and sobering experience.

Not having the work to support myself, I had to find a way to support myself. I had to eliminate all unnecessary costs, wherever I could. My family and I had to find somewhere less expensive to live, we couldn't eat out anymore, we couldn't travel anymore. It was becoming more and more difficult to be able to pay bills. I could barely make my payments for the simplest of things, like the water bill. So, let's go back to having to find new and different ways to support myself.

After a lot of searching, I was turned onto Network Marketing. I'd had some experience watching my Mom being in network marketing groups, with two of the biggest names in the industry. Being able to grow a team, make your own hours, take off when you want to, and still make some good money. This was what I wanted.

Now, mind you, over the years, I have been in some great businesses and some....let's say, not so great. I have learned and gleaned SO much information about the network marketing industry as a whole, how it works, who to rub shoulders with and who 'not' to rub shoulders with, if you know what I mean.

Network marketing as an industry is a multi-billion dollar industry. And what a great model that it could be for one to gain success. I was hooked. I wanted to know all there was about how it all worked and how I could grow a team and myself in the process.

As I stated earlier, I have been in some great companies in the network marketing field. I have met CEOs, Board of Directors, and Executives with the same VISION that I have had all of these years---to grow myself as an entrepreneur. As I was growing in the network marketing industry, moving from company to company, trying to find a home for myself with one of them, I'd thought that I had. Sadly, I was wrong. There can tend to be a lot of deception in the Corporate world and Network Marketing is not immune to it. After losing my entire team, friends that I considered family, I had the painful decision to make. It was time to move on from this particular company. I learned so much from the higher ups in the company, but one thing that I learned most of all, was who I can trust.

I have always believed that everything is connected. God has a plan for all of us in this world and this was just a speed bump in that I needed to get over and move forward, into momentum and find something else to do.

I have always read, "NEVER GIVE UP-----NEVER." And also, "Fall Down Seven Times, Get up Eight." Those are great quotes to not giving up on your vision.

I cried for a solid week over what had happened. I had fallen into a severe depression and was asking myself "WHY ME, Lord?"

And then, for a second time in my life, I had contemplated suicide. I had felt that God had forsaken me. Thankfully, through a lot of prayer (and a lot of Xanax), God spoke to me through an amazing book by Andy Andrews, called "The Traveller's Gift." It was this book that I reflected back upon during this dark & negative time in my life, and prayed and prayed for God to remove these dark thoughts from my life.

I am so grateful that God did remove those dark thoughts from me that I was having. It was then that I found another very special book. It is "Jesus Calling." This is a daily devotional book, is written as if Jesus is speaking directly to me the support, guidance and encouragement that I needed in my life. This book REALLY has caused me to step back and take a very long look at my own life, where I have been, where I am at, and where I am headed.

I am so thankful to God for directing me to this book, as it has really enabled me to experience a deeper, personal relationship with the Him. It was here that I picked myself up and prayed to Him, sometimes in tears, asking for Him to bless me with wisdom, knowledge, & understanding (as King Solomon did). I knew that these far outweighed asking for riches. I knew that God was in control of everything, and would bless me as He saw fit. One thing that I always have to remember is that it had to be in HIS time, NOT my own.

Since, I have grown spiritually, in this way, throwing ALL of my cares at His feet and asking for wisdom, knowledge and understanding, I have been blessed beyond measure. All of my businesses have exploded. I have had connections that I have not spoken to in over 10 years contact me to work on their project. It feels so good to be busy again, after 7 years of lean times.

Being able to help those people that were not necessarily blessed with a creative vision feels so good. Being able to map out on paper a vision of what someone's dream is, sometimes gives me chills. I am now looking at different ways to grow myself. I am venturing out into different fields, other than architecture. I learned that having multiple streams of income was the key to my future success. Yes, it would mean a lot of sacrifice over the years, but, the end result would be worth it.

Other ventures that I am looking into are Binary Options, FOREX Trading, opening a retail business (secret for now), and investing into the rental Real Estate Market, all while continuing on, here and there, with my main/two businesses. Lately, my mind has been racing about, with different thoughts about how I can reinvent myself yet again, to create, inspire, and grow.

God has blessed us with a brain. Let's use that gift to find new and different ways to become prosperous with Entrepreneurship. God wants us to be prosperous. Look at what Matthew 6:33 says, *"But seek first the kingdom of God, and his righteousness; and all these things shall be added to you."* It is a promise of God to bless you, if you seek Him first.

If I can offer anything to those of you reading this, that are looking to embark on becoming an entrepreneur, I would say, _Believe in Yourself_ and what you have to offer. _Grow_, by immersing yourself in self-development books. _Put your trust in God_, and He will direct your path that you are on. _Condition your mind for a higher productivity_ and do more with what you have been given.

I am truly blessed and living in Abundance and Gratitude right now and so excited about where my path is headed.

What are you going to do, to GROW your future self?

3

God's Plan Is Always Better Than Your Plan!
Andrea "Dre" Nichols Everett

● ● ●

My father has been an entrepreneur for almost my entire life. I saw how hard he worked and how well he provided for my family but I never dreamed of following in his entrepreneurial footsteps. I actually always dreamed of becoming an attorney. I was always drawn to the idea of justice for all and helping people who could not help themselves. But the dream of becoming an attorney never came to fruition because it was my plan for my life and not God's plan for my life. When I allowed God to direct my path, He led me to an entrepreneurial path. It was also God's dream for me to help others, but not in the way that I had planned. He has provided me with the opportunity to help people live stronger and healthier lives all while creating a legacy for my family as an entrepreneur.

How It All Began...
After graduating from the University of Virginia in 1993, I was not quite sure what I wanted to do with my life. I

thought I wanted to go to law school eventually, but I honestly needed some time off from all things school for a while so I could regroup and then refocus to continue my education. I decided to start working at USAir in Charlottesville, VA because I thought that would be a great way for me to see the world seeing that all employees were able to fly for free. While at USAir, I learned fantastic customer service skills and was able to decompress after 4 tough years in college. Although the money was not great because I only worked part time, I had it made because my parents were sending me money on a regular basis to help cover my expenses. Talk about living a dream life! Well, that was until about a year later when my parents told me that they would no longer subsidize my income unless I was going to go to law school. They told me that I needed to "grow up" and decide what I really wanted to do with my life. Dang, it was now time for me to jump into real adulthood.

I knew I was not ready to start school again so I quit my job at USAir and got a job as an Assistant Manager of Chico's, a women's clothing store in Charlottesville. The job was great because the money allowed me to sustain a decent lifestyle, without my parents' support, and I was learning management skills. After about 2 years at Chico's, I decided it was time for me to move on. I decided on a career in HR/temporary staffing because I was eager to learn more about managing people. I really enjoyed this job because I was able to connect people with great jobs. I felt like I was starting to make a difference in this world. However, during these first few years out of college working in the "real world", I never made time for exercise. I just did not *feel* like it so it was never a priority of mine.

By June of 1995, I met a beautiful man in a Kroger grocery store in Charlottesville, VA. He was the store Manager and he was just an amazing and kind man. We fell in love and as so many couples do, we started eating and eating and eating. Although he played basketball occasionally, we both were not consistently active so we both began to gain weight.

By Sept of 1997, that grocery store Manager asked me to marry him and we soon relocated to Raleigh, NC to start our lives together. About six months before my wedding, I started to work out because I wanted to look really fabulous on my wedding day. Since I always loved step aerobics, I knew I could take 5 or 6 step classes a week and lose about 15 pounds, fairly quickly. Well, I achieved my goal and I got into my dream-sized wedding dress for my October 1998 wedding day. However, after the honeymoon, I drifted back into my old unhealthy sedentary habits. I never really enjoyed exercise so it was easy for me to stop, especially since my goal had already been achieved.

The first 6 months of my marriage were filled with eating and drinking anything and everything I wanted. My husband and I both had very stressful careers so we would often unwind by going out to dinner and indulging in rich food options and calorie laden alcoholic beverages. We were truly enjoying our newlywed status to the utmost and gaining weight without even realizing it.

This carefree lifestyle came to an abrupt end in April 1999. Let's face it, losing weight, exercising regularly, and adopting a healthy diet is hard to maintain. So, I believe that in order to start living a healthy lifestyle you have to hit your "rock bottom." Your "rock bottom" is when you are so uncomfortable with your current habits that the pain of remaining the same is greater than the pain of change. I reached my rock bottom in a dressing room in Stein Mart clothing store.

My Rock Bottom...

Because I was always so busy at work, I rarely found time to go shopping for myself. Well, one Saturday afternoon I decided to go out and buy myself some new work clothes. I hadn't gone shopping in months so I was excited to see what the new fashions were in my favorite store, at that time it was Stein Mart. Now, back in 1999, the style was to wear the long maxi style knit skirts and dresses that had the elastic band around the waist and were very forgiving of all rolls and extra pounds one might carry. I actually had about 15 of these skirts in all different styles and colors. I loved them because they were professional looking and made you look very slim and fit. But the downside to wearing elastic band skirts and dresses is that they are stretchy knit material so you really do not know what size you are since the skirts allow you to expand without realizing you are expanding! I will never forget how I felt the moment I tried to put my hips in a pair of jeans that were not stretchy and had no elastic waist! That is where my rock bottom began.

Ok, so I was super excited about going to Stein Mart to finally get some new clothes! I was so ready to purchase some new clothing that I actually grabbed about 10 dresses, several suits and a few pairs of jeans for fun. Now, I typically do not try on clothing in stores because I really do not like being undressed in those dressing rooms because they make me feel so vulnerable. But, I decided to step outside of my comfort zone and try on the items I had selected. At the time, I didn't realize how this one decision could change my life forever.

I entered the dressing room and decided to try on the jeans because they were really cute and trendy looking. I put the jeans on and I could not get them over my hips. I immediately thought, *Oh, they have these jeans marked incorrectly. They are a size smaller than they are marked.* So, I asked the saleswoman to please find me a pair in the correct size because I just knew that I was around a size 7/8 or at the most a 9/10 and not an 11/12. Well, she came back with the new jeans and once again I could not get them over my hips. That is when panic set in. I looked at myself in the mirror and thought, *How did this happen—how did you allow yourself to get this big?* Some of you may be thinking, a 9/10 is not a big size at all; but if you have been a 5/6 or 7/8 the majority of your life and then you are a 9/10 or possibly an 11/12, that is big to you and it's shocking. To put it mildly, I totally had a meltdown in that dressing room. I felt fat and ugly and I just wanted to go home. I remember running out of the dressing room, leaving all the items I had brought in and crying all the way home. I was so disappointed in myself and I just felt miserable.

So, what do all women who feel miserable and fat do to make themselves feel better? e eat...and that is exactly what I did. I went home, got in my bed, turned on Lifetime TV and started to eat a bag of Cool Ranch Doritos with grape Kool-Aid. Yep, sure did! I wanted to eat my feelings away as quickly as possible.

My Transformation Moment...
As I was watching some sorry sappy Lifetime movie, a commercial for The YMCA came on and I was immediately intrigued. I sat up and watched the commercial and I honestly felt like God was speaking to me through the commercial. As soon as the commercial ended, I jumped up, threw away the Doritos and the Kool-Aid and changed into an exercise bra and some really short shorts. I then asked my husband to take a picture of me, front, back and side view. I hung the pictures on my bathroom mirror because I decided, at that very moment, that I was never going to look and feel that way again. I decided that this was my rock bottom and I refused to ever get to this place again. The very next day I signed up to join the AE Finley YMCA in Raleigh, NC and I have never looked back!

The Beginning of Dre (My Fierce Alter Ego)
I started my exercise journey at the YMCA by making myself a priority. Because I worked such long hours at my job, I told my boss that it was very important to me to leave work by 5:30pm on Mondays and Wednesdays because I wanted to make it to my step and weight-

lifting classes at The Y. He was very supportive and my journey to a fit body began. I started off attending just 2 classes a week but as I started to see results, I added classes and days until I was up to 5 or 6 days per week. I started to LOVE working out and the way it made me feel. My clothes were getting bigger and bigger and I had so much amazing energy all the time.

One day when I was in my step class, I had an epiphany. As the music was playing I realized that I really did not like the type of music this instructor was using for her workouts. I realized that if I were an instructor, I would play the best music to keep all my participants engaged throughout the entire workout because the music fuels the workout. That very night I decided that I wanted to become a part time fitness instructor. That very night changed my life forever.

I studied to get my Group Fitness Instructor certificate and immediately started teaching classes at The Y and all over Raleigh within 6 months. I decided that if I was going to be an instructor, I needed a "stage name". I decided to call my alter Fitness Instructor ego "Dre" because it was short for Andrea, it sounded kind of bad ass, and it was easy to remember. So, Dre was born!

I soon taught myself how to teach kick boxing, step aerobics, weight lifting classes and cycle classes. I also fell in love with learning new exercise disciplines and I earned certification after certification so I could always stay current with all things fitness. I was so eager to learn and to become the best instructor, I could possibly be. I wanted to help people feel the way I felt about my new body and being an instructor really helped me inspire change in others.

As a new instructor, when you go to audition for a class at a gym, the Fitness Director may give you a class at the toughest time slot on the schedule to fill. It may be 8pm which is a difficult time slot to fill up in fitness. Well, every time I was given a difficult time slot to fill, I filled it to capacity within a few weeks. I absolutely loved being an instructor and my classes could feel that love and passion. That is when I knew that I had a God-given gift for fitness. That is when I knew that I had to eventually do something on a bigger scale than just part-time classes-- but I just didn't know what it was yet. But when I moved to Chicago, God was ready for me to know the next plans He had for my life.

The Birth of D3
My family is very close. We are a smaller family, but we really enjoy living close to each other because our bond is so strong. I was born in Chicago, but I grew up from the age of 4 in Meriden, CT. My parents and sister moved back to Chicago in 2002 and although I loved living in Raleigh, I knew that I would eventually move back to Chicago as well.

In Feb 2003, my husband and I moved to Chicago after we both got new positions in pharmaceutical sales. When I first arrived in Chicago, I started attending different fitness classes to feel out how the Chicago fitness instructors taught classes. I attended 10 to 15 different classes and I was very impressed with their skills but I knew that I was as good, if not better, than most of the instructors (not to toot my own horn but once you become an entrepreneur, you have to learn to give yourself props because no else will—I mean, you are your boss, right?). So, without hesitation, I started auditioning for several different gyms in the Chicagoland area. Once I started booking classes, I worked on building my core followers at each gym. I taught at 4 gyms on the north side of Chicago and I fell in love with all my classes and by the grace of God, I am pretty sure they fell in love with me too. Although my pharmaceutical career was very successful, I absolutely loved my time in front of my fitness classes. Teaching aerobics just gave me life! It was what, I believe, I was created to do!

And then calamity struck! My mother had polycystic kidney disease and I was the only person in my family who was healthy and fit enough to give her the kidney she desperately needed. So, in February of 2006, I gave my mother my left kidney and saved her life. The surgery went perfectly and we both recovered over the next several weeks. However, after the surgery, I felt a shift in my spirit. I felt a need to do more and give more. God made me feel like He was speaking directly to me and He was saying: "Get out there and do more." I did not know what that meant, but He slowly started to show me that He had something bigger and better for my life. He started revealing it to me in May of 2006 with a simple request from a friend.

A friend of mine was getting married in the fall of 2006 and asked if I would lead a boot camp with her and her 4 bridesmaids. I was excited about the opportunity because I loved instructing and I loved the idea of not working for a gym because I could do everything my way for a change! We began having classes at the track across the street from my house in May of 2006. Well, by the end of the summer, I had about 15 boot campers because people would see us on the track and wanted to join us. As the weather started to get colder, I ended the boot camp and told them we would all start again in the spring of 2007. Everyone was disappointed but we did not have an indoor space to use for workout sessions so the classes ended and that was that. I never even thought about continuing on as a business because I was doing very well in my full-time sales position and, honestly, I never dreamed of owning my own business...not yet, at least.

In the spring of 2007, I was starting to feel very unfulfilled in pharmaceutical sales Even though I was #1 in the country in sales and had recently won the highly coveted Presidents Council Award, which is the top award in pharmaceutical sales, I still felt empty inside. I am not sure what I was searching for but I just wanted something different. Looking back, I now know that the empty feeling was God's way of telling me that it was time for my next phase. And my next phase involved a book, a doctor, a reverend, and a whole lot of faith.

The Secret Revealed...
I would often DVR The Oprah Winfrey Show and watch it in the morning before I headed out to my sales territory. It was kind of like a ritual for me because she just really inspired me to be the best I could be while I was out in my sales territory. One morning I was watching her show

on the book called *The Secret*. I can remember being totally mesmerized by the guests who were discussing how you can have and be anything you want if you focus on the positive vibes of the universe, trust it and have faith that you can do anything you want to do. Was this the secret to success? Did I just have to believe I could do anything and it would happen if I put forth the effort?

I was instantly hooked! I purchased the book and created my very first vision board. According to *The Secret*, you create a vision board with everything you want to achieve or obtain in life. I created my board and I added Oprah to the very center of the board because I wanted to one day work at Harpo Studios.

I decided it was time for me to start doing what I loved to do on a bigger level. It was time for me to trust the universe to provide me with what I needed to be successful. I wanted to get my boot camp started again for the spring and really try to grow it because I knew I was really helping people get fit and feel better. Now, at this time, I was not really thinking about holding the classes past the summer months but that is not the plan God had for me.

In order to get started, I called all my boot campers from the previous year and told them that we would meet 2 times a week at the beach off Lake Shore Drive in Chicago. I knew that if I was in a public place, I would get more visibility and more people would want to join. By the end of the summer, I had a 6am class and a 5pm, 6pm, and 7pm class three nights a week and each class was packed. I had to stop teaching at all the gyms where I led classes because the boot camp just took off like crazy. But again, I was only thinking the classes would last until October, at the latest, and then we would restart in the spring. Well, that was the case until one of my members asked me what we were going to do when it got cold outside. I thought about it for a second and a thought flashed through my mind. What if I got a space and continued on with this idea? What if I could actually make this a real business? Could I do this?

Anytime I need guidance on any big decision, I ask my father because he always tells me the truth (whether I want to hear it or not ☺) and he offers the best advice. I called my dad and after I explained my dilemma, he asked me one question: "Do you love it?" When I answered in the affirmative, he told me that I could make a business out of anything I loved. That was the day D3: Dre's Diesel Dome Fitness, LLC was born.

Trusting The Secret...
After I spoke with my father, I remember, I pulled my car over to the side of the road and I asked God if this was the direction He wanted for my life. I asked Him to make it "all right or make it all wrong" so I would clearly know the direction I should go. I asked the Lord to lay it down "like butter" if I was supposed to make D3 a real business. And, that is exactly what HE did for me. Now, do not get me wrong, I have had my share of ups and downs building this business, but when I first started it, God made sure I had many more ups than downs because this is what He had for me.

My first step in building my new business was to look for a safe, affordable, and warm space for my clients. One of my doctors told me about a gym space off of Michigan Ave in a church. I went and checked out the gym and it was in horrible condition but I knew I could clean it up for my classes. I met with the Reverend and we negotiated a price for the rent and I was officially in business.

The gym space was really in bad shape. One day, while I was in my sales territory, I was telling one of my doctors, who had become rather like a grandfather to me over the years, that I had this space to start my side business but it looked really awful. He told me that he wanted to come and see the space because he wanted to support my dream. I was so surprised at his response and decided to show him the space. He walked in and told me that he wanted to gut and remodel the gym for me because he believed I could help so many people live longer happier lives. I was floored and so very excited. At first I told him that I could not accept it but he would not take no for an answer and absolutely insisted. Wow, right? Remember when I told you I asked God to "lay it down like butter" for me? Well, if that isn't butter, I do not know what is! We were able to move into my gym space a few months later. Thank you Dr. Smith!

As I was building D3, I was also still working in my full-time sales position for Eli Lilly Pharmaceutical. In pharmaceutical sales, there is a lot of flexible time that you can do your own thing and run your territory, however, I never did D3 work on Lilly's time clock. I was a firm believer of giving the company the time I owed it on a daily basis. I truly believed God would not bless D3 if I cheated Lilly by working D3 on their time. It was so hard for me because I was really working 2 full-time jobs. I was working all day in the field for Lilly and then I was working all night up until 2 am and 3 am for D3. And believe it or not, as I was working so hard, I won the President's Council Award at Lilly for the 2nd year in a row and my territory remained #1 in the country for 2 consecutive years (2007 and 2008). It just goes to show, that if you work hard, you can absolutely achieve anything in life.

By June of 2008, I was exhausted. D3 was running 20 classes a week and I had very little help and I knew it was time for me to make some serious changes. I finally took a leap of faith and left my full-time sales position at Eli Lilly and Co. that very month. I left at the top of my game and many people could not believe I would quit a job where I was making lots of money and had the potential to move up quickly. But what they did not know was that I was following God's lead for my life. I was listening to the inner voice inside of me and that inner voice told me it was time to spread my wings and reach for my dreams. That was the best day of my life because I started to walk in faith and no longer in fear. And with that official resignation, D3 had my full attention and it started to soar!

Finally On My Way...
Eight years later, I have learned so much. I have made hundreds of mistakes and I have made hundreds of really good decisions. I love the life I have created for myself and I would not change one struggle I have

endured for it. I finally have a fantastic team supporting me and we have all built an incredible culture at D3. D3 has evolved into more of a group fitness boutique rather than just a boot camp. We also now have several programs to teach our members how to get in shape and stay in shape.

As D3 has grown over the years, I have been blessed to be featured in Jet Magazine, Ebony Magazine, and numerous other Chicago-based newspapers. ABC News and 190 North have featured D3 live on air. D3 has also received numerous leadership and community awards.

But the best part about my journey is not all the accolades. The best part is actually looking back at my life and seeing how God aligned everything I ever did to get me where I am today—helping thousands of people get in shape and live longer stronger lives. I now see that everything I have ever done was based on God laying down HIS plan for my life. I was in management at Chico's to develop my management skills. I was in HR to learn about how to staff my company. I was in sales to help me with my selling skills and I taught fitness because that is what God has made my ministry to touch and transform lives. It feels so good to know why I am here. I am finally fulfilled.

Law School— EPIC FAIL!
So you are probably wondering what happened to my law school aspirations? Well, I applied to several law schools and was denied due to the fact that my LSAT scores were too low. I took many different LSAT prep

classes, but my scores were always the same. For some reasons, I typically bomb on those standardize tests.

I did, however, manage to get into a conditional program at John Marshall Law School in 2006 which was a program that allowed you to take summer law school courses to see if you had what it took to be accepted. When I first started the program, I asked God to lead me and direct me. I asked Him to "make it all right or make it all wrong". Well, I kicked butt in all my classes but when it came time for me to take the tests, I FAILED miserably. Even though I studied and knew all the answers, I completely froze up in the exams. I was devastated at the time. Why did God make it ALL wrong? Then I realized He made it ALL wrong because it truly was ALL wrong for my life. I now know law school was just not FOR me and what God had FOR me was so much better. Goes to show, sometimes an epic fail can lead you to a successful sail!

The Reality of Being An Entrepreneur...
You hear often that being an entrepreneur is the toughest yet most rewarding thing you can ever do with your life...and I agree. It's so awesome to be your own boss and have total control of your life, but with that freedom comes massive responsibility. The reality of it all is actually very overwhelming at times.

Think about it like this, owning a business is like having a baby that never really grows up. I mean, it grows but you have to continue to put your optimal effort into it even though it is getting older. With children, you help them grow up and equip them to eventually care for themselves. With a business, you must always care for it and nurture it because the moment you slack, you could lose it.

I really want to be very honest with you. Please do not think I am trying to talk you out of achieving your dreams but you really have to be ready for anything when you own a business. I have actually had some very bleak and dark times where I wanted to quit and go back to Corporate America where I was sure to get a paycheck every month. There have been times that I was just burned out to the ground and could not work at all. I have had tough financial times that scared me to death. But, I always knew that if I just persevered, I would be able to make it to the other side. And I always have.

With the bad times, there have been many exciting and fabulous times. Remember I told you about my vision board? Well, I put Oprah in the middle of it and about 6 months after I started working D3 full-time, I was asked to audition to be a trainer for Harpo Studios...and I got it! I worked at Harpo for 4 years and I even got to go on their Trip of a Lifetime Cruise. Talk about a win! I will never forget speaking with Oprah for the first time. In my mind I kept thinking: *Why you? Why are you speaking to the most powerful woman in the world?* And then I stopped myself and said: *Why not me?* In that moment, I realized that I could do and be anything I set my mind to do. Speaking with Oprah empowered me and took my life and my business to the next level. God always gives you what you need to carry on His work.

My Advice To Budding Entrepreneurs...

Reality Check: 8 Things You Need To Ask Yourself Before You Start Your Business:

Do you LOVE what you do and would you do it for free? If you are not totally in love with what you are building then you will not last. If you would not do what you "do" for free—then you need to think twice about starting your own business.

Do you realize your business is not about what you do but rather how you market it? Many beginner entrepreneurs think that when they go into business that they will be working on what they "do" to build their companies. Now, what you "do" is important and you need to be very good at it but your main responsibility is how you **market** what you "do". If you do not learn how to market and sell your services, you will be "doing" what you "do" alone.

Are you really prepared to sow before you reap? When you first get started building your company/brand, you will be working countless and thankless hours with little to no reward. You need to be disciplined and tough enough to create the foundation of your business through sheer hard work and determination. You may or may not see the results you want or expect for years but just know that over time, if you do not quit, you will eventually get to reap the benefits of your hard work.

Are you willing to give up relationships and your current lifestyle to fulfill your dream?

Most people in your life will not will not understand your passion and drive to build your brand so as you are focusing on your business, you will probably start to lose friends. Starting a business takes up your entire life. You will be totally consumed and hyper focused on your work so you will have less and less time to spend with friends and family. It's sad, but it's true. However, remember this, the friends you don't lose are your friends for life.

Are you financially prepared for this new venture—how is your credit score? Make sure you have all your financial ducks in a row because you will eventually need financing to grow your business. If you do not have excellent credit, make it a priority to raise your credit score so you can apply for loans if necessary. Remember, it takes money to make money so do not be afraid to get the funding you need to advance your company. Make sure you research all of the different funding source available before you choose a financial institution. There are thousands of options out there so do your research and don't just jump at the first dollar thrown your way.

Do you know what the important numbers are in your business? If you are like me, I did not have a business background per se. I didn't know anything about a profit and loss sheets, balance sheets or profit margins, etc. I was never a numbers person so I was very intimidated by these concepts. My first 3 years in business, I really had no idea what my numbers meant. I literally thought that if I had money in the bank, I was good to go. Crazy right? But you would be surprised at how many entrepreneurs run their companies without knowing those numbers. Take the time to understand your market and the important numbers for your business. If you don't understand the numbers, then you don't understand the health of your business.

Is your business protected using the correct entity and is your legal team in place? Be sure to register your business as an LLC, C-Corp, S-Corp or other business entity. Consult with an attorney to see what entity works best for what you are trying to accomplish. You need to protect yourself and your business.

So you have your business model and business plan ready? Make sure you create a viable business plan and model from the beginning. You must have a plan to get to the next phase. If you do not have a plan, you are really planning to fail.

Do you speak with God? If you don't, start. He is the answer to all your problems. If you have noticed, I ask God all the time to "make it all right or make it all wrong" when I am looking to make a move in my life. Believe me, He always answers that prayer and makes the answer crystal clear. Just be prepared to listen because He may make it "all wrong" and that simply means, it's not for you.

Summary

The Good News And The Bad News About Starting Your Own Biz...

The bad news first. Starting a business deems understanding that you must LOVE what you do in order to be successful. I say this because your business will become your child and you must love and nurture your child to be successful. You have to be willing to work over 100 hours a week in order for your business to start making any traction. Know that the more time and effort you put into your business, the more you will get in return. You may go years and years before you reach any type of true success but if you are persistent, like I have mentioned before, you will eventually reap what you sow.

Now for the good news, as you are going through the struggles of building your business, you are creating your story. Your story is the beautiful evolution of your business. Everything you do, whether it be good or bad, is part of your journey. Cherish everything you go through because those "ups and downs" are all about building your dream. They are YOUR story.

So, I leave you with one quote by Henry Ford: "If you think you can do a thing or think you can't do a thing, you are right." Don't allow the fear of success or the fear of failure to stop you from trying. If God places the thought in your mind, He will give you what you need to be successful. Trust me, I know.

Dre Nichols-Everett, The Exercise Habit Coach

D3: Dre's Diesel Dome Fitness, LLC

Live in Chicago? Try a free class here:
www.d3getfit.com

Want to learn to make exercise a habit and get free resources and helpful weight loss and nutrition courses? Go here: www.exercisehabitcoach.com

4

To Have and to Hold, from this *Business* Forward
Carrie Elaine Forman

•••

Owning your own business is like being in a relationship. Relationships need attention, passion, dedication, trust and commitment in order to be successful. So does your business. I'm sure if you're like me you have either experienced or witnessed a relationship that started off great but over time things like disrespect, neglect, lack of trust and the normal daily stresses of life began to "chip away" at the foundation of that relationship. Your business can also suffer from these circumstances if it's not given consistent commitment and passion.

Loving What You Do
Being in love is such an amazing feeling! It took me 40 years to experience that feeling and when I finally did...WOW! Besides my Creator, my husband, Victor keeps my spirit on HIGH. I love to love him. There's not much work involved and the rewards are amazing! I've also experienced true love with my business (finally) after learning that loving what I do is the key. There is

such a great difference between having your own business and having a job. Most times, people go to a job because it pays the bills. If they had a choice and money wasn't an option, they probably wouldn't work there. Being an entrepreneur and owning your own business is voluntary. You don't HAVE to show up, you CHOOSE to show up. The fear or possibility of someone firing you is no longer an issue. Now, do you choose to show up because you feel you HAVE to or do you show up because you love it?

My point is that your business needs your love. It's hard for me to pick out just one of my favorite things about the business Victor and I have built together. I love it all! I love working with people, branding and marketing and even customer support and shipping. None of it seems like "work" to me. In order to stay committed and having a consistent belief and value in your company, you need to genuinely love it! It shouldn't be just about the money (reward), as the reward will naturally come AFTER all the right verbs are put into action (commitment/dedication/ belief). And there is one guarantee...if you are an entrepreneur then you are in the people business. Whether you are selling a product, service or idea, you are selling it to a person.

So in addition to loving what you do, you have to genuinely love people. People can sense if you believe in and love your company. They can sense if you love what you do. They will naturally be drawn to you as a result of your visible confidence in what you represent because of your LOVE for it. Think about those who love to grow a garden. Yes, there is work involved with preparing the right soil, planting, watering consistently, pulling out the weeds, etc. But for those that love to garden, is it considered **hard** work? I believe it's considered Passionate work. Every gardener I know loves it! It's their escape... It's their passion. They have so much joy tending to the plants and watching them bloom and sowing seeds and reaping the reward later. That is exactly how the "work" should feel with a healthy relationship and with a healthy business.

So, if you don't love it...don't do it. Find out WHO you are first and then do what you love.

Harmony and Purpose
As I stated above, Victor and I work together. Having a spouse as a business partner (we call this a "spartner") is a great advantage for many reasons but it can also hurt your business if you and your spartner are not equally yoked. It can be tricky IF you have different agenda's and personalities. It's very important that you identify and communicate your visions and goals in order to move forward successfully.

Victor and I work so well together because we have communicated clearly about our goals: our expectations to reach those goals while staying focused on them, just as the gardener has the goal of having a prosperous garden.

We encourage you to sit down with your spartner and talk about your goals and dreams. Why are you both doing this business? And be specific. Call us crazy but we have a goal to own a castle in Europe. We even shop online and print off our favorites. It helps us stay focused on why we work so hard each day. We also planned out our retirement month and year. We can clearly envision what our life will be like when we retire and begin enjoying the "fruits" from our labor.

If sitting down with your spartner and planning out goals becomes a challenge, then maybe re-think going into business with them.

For example, if you are a dreamer and imagine reaching for the stars, having a luxurious lifestyle, traveling the world, helping others, etc... but your spartner just wants to pay the bills and couldn't care less about all that other stuff, then there's a problem. Going into business with them might not be the best route, as it will hurt your relationship and your business. You are only as strong as your weakest link. So paying the bills might be as far as you get.

Therefore, sit down with your spartner ASAP and plan your life. Having the finish line specifically drawn out helps you run towards it as "passionate work" and not "hard work." Staying focused on those goals daily also helps you keep running because you're reminded that the finish line looks so good.

Flourishing in Your Roles

Now that you've mapped out your finish line with your spartner, it's time to determine who runs when, where and how fast. There are many departments in even small businesses. There's marketing, branding, IT, accounting, customer support, and so on. Identifying both of your strengths, weaknesses and roles are very important to know who is assigned to what tasks.

I love to listen to Victor play the piano. He has been playing since he was a kid and he is so good at it. Anytime there is a piano around, even in a hotel lobby... I can't wait for him to do his thing. I, on the other hand, have absolutely no talent on the piano and if I started any attempt to play, people would be covering their ears and running away.

So how silly would it be for me to say "Victor, I got this, let me take over." and start attempting to play something that would hopefully sound like music? It's the same with your roles. Identify each other's strengths and talents and embrace your role. One person might be very creative and outgoing. The other, analytical and may be driven by numbers. Learning your personality type (what motivates you) is important.

For example, I'm "Mrs. Social"! I love having fun, working with people, and am always thinking of new ideas, slogans and I have no problem shouting "Cülbeans!" on the rooftops (that's our company). So my role is marketing, branding, and working with our field of affiliates. Victor has a natural talent for marketing as well but also has to be on top of reports, data and keeping the books or he doesn't sleep well at night! I couldn't care less about financial reports or data...just let me design a t-shirt, hee hee! So there is no doubt that we have the best person in place as CFO. He loves it and there is no question it's done right. I don't try to do his role and he lets me run free in mine!

Balance – Have a Life Outside of Your Business

One of the biggest mistakes I've made for many years in my entrepreneurial career is having my business run my life rather than me running my business. I lost many quality years and special moments with family that I can never get back, mainly because I was chasing money. If you're consistently chasing the money, it will consistently keep running from you. This is where TIME MANAGEMENT is essential. Just as I spoke about commitment and dedication before, it should all fit nice-n-snug in a window of time. For example, if you have committed to 7 hours a day to your business then give 120% during those 7 hours. Do not get side-tracked. Then at the 7-hour mark, shut it off! Now spend the rest of that day's time with your family and friends.

I have witnessed others who are disturbingly unbalanced in their life (which used to be me). Their business owns every part of them. It's sad for me to see because I strongly believe when this particular business owner have finally reached their definition of success, they will have no one to share it with. They will be alone in their riches. In my opinion, there is nothing richer than the combining of two prosperities...

(1) relationships with special people and (2) the ability to enjoy financial freedom with those special people.

Having a balanced life is also important for your sanity and happiness. You will enjoy your business more when it doesn't own you, but you own it. Victor and I make a point to shut it off every evening and on Saturdays. We then terribly miss it and can't wait to jump on our computers when our "work window" starts up again. I feel my brain is fresh, polished and I'm much more creative with a clear head. So, just as a prosperous garden needs a balance of rain and sun, so does your life. Enjoy that dedicated window of time that you spend in your business. And just as well, enjoy that dedicated window of time with your family and friends. Just be sure that during that dedicated time, you give it your all! Not 50%, not even 75%...but 120% of you should go into that dedicated time. Your business will appreciate it, your family will appreciate it and next thing you know...you have a prosperous garden. So, in the spirit of gardening... when you discover your passion... ***bloom where you're planted.***

5

Build your BRAND, start a LEGACY!
Vau've A. Davis

Build your BRAND with your LEGACY in mind. I believe your brand's legacy should be driven by your passion to succeed and leave something behind for those who follow in your footsteps. Your brand is more than a business, a slogan or logo.

• • •

"There are lots of bad reasons to start a company. But there's only one good, legitimate reason, and I think you know what it is: it's to change the world."
- Phil Libin, CEO of Evernote.

What's Your Why?
As a first generation entrepreneur, I aspire to build a legacy through business development and community service. I have a deep passion for helping develop and serve our communities. My WHY is and has always been to leave a legacy and to inspire others to live a life of purpose through service. I currently own a PR consulting firm where I've assisted in elevating the brands of local entrepreneurs, small businesses and non-profits to national levels as well as give back to the community. Through Official Anais PR we counsel clients on ways to

use their professional platforms to create legacies that will make a difference long after their gone.

One will find that Official Anais PR does a great deal of community service and it's done in hopes that we inspire YOU. Our lead Graphic and Website specialist, Brian Wyatt, also uses his services to give back, specifically to the Veterans. Giving back is vitally important to us and our brand's mission, collectively and independently.

I'm currently building my personal brand, "Vau've Anais", which is highly focused on philanthropy, community organizing, fundraising and volunteer recruitment. No matter what I decide to do professionally, there will be something that leads to service or giving back. Service and giving back is what I would like my life legacy to be and inspire others to do.

As a first generation entrepreneur and college graduate I want to build something for my family to be proud of. I want to inspire others to do their part in their communities. I'm driven to leave my stamp on the world through helping others through resource development, philanthropy and community service.

2: WHY/HOW/WHEN DID YOU PURSUE YOUR BUSINESS

Your brand is your ministry.

Starting a business is much like starting a family....there is never a perfect time.

I actually started my business during one of the most difficult times of my life. During that time I came to the conclusion that I would need to monetize my ability to "connect the dots. I've always been coined the connector and it's that talent that led me to start Official Anais PR Firm on 10/10/10. I never thought of it as my first business, a branding platform or even a main stream of income. I just knew I loved helping others through my resourcefulness. In an effort to build my own legacy, my company assists others in building their brand to create their own legacies. Our target demographic is primarily small businesses, entrepreneurs and non-for-profits.

We just celebrated four years last fall. Initially, we provided PR services such as media kits, press releases and social media management. As of 2014, we solely consult clients. It's been a rewarding journey the last four years. I literally taught myself everything I know about public relations and marketing. I took notes from mentors and there were some things that were trial and error (some of the best learning experiences come this way).

By no means was PR my "hobby" but I had a gift for using my resourcefulness to help others. Building a brand and business is not one in the same. If you are looking to START a business there are countless resources to help you start the rigorous process of sharpening your skills and making a profit. However, I've found that BUILDING a brand is a little more personal and it will follow you beyond any services rendered. You can always opt to sell your business and start a new venture but building a brand becomes a part of your identity. I find this true even more so now given that social media handles are like the new phone number. I believe your brand is highly driven by your PURPOSE in life and that is ultimately a part of God's will for our lives.

I think those that believe in a higher power find (some discover later than others) that their career endeavors are greatly shaped by their passion which is usually a gift that God has given us to build our ministry.

3: TIPS FOR ELEVATING, SUCCESS, INSPIRATION, GROWTH + PUSHING THROUGH

"Watch, listen, and learn. You can't know it all yourself. Anyone who thinks they do is destined for mediocrity." - **Donald Trump**, *chairman of The Trump Organization, the Trump Plaza Associates, LLC.*

Find someone or people that you can confide in about ANYTHING!

Take advantage of all the free resources you can get your hands on prior to investing in seminars, classes and conferences. Those funds can be used to invest in other things that you need to get started as a legitimate professional business owner. Often time's people are so excited about "launching" that they overlook some of the basics or don't want to wait. An example of this would be:

Website/vanity email
Marketing Materials

Advertising (tangible products)

HUSTLE and Have Patience!

I would suggest that any aspiring entrepreneur read, Thrive: 30 Inspirational Rags to Riches Stories. It will help inspire you and keep you motivated during those times you feel like you can't catch a break.

Network

A great deal of my network has grown from simply networking across the city, via social media and outside of my comfort zone (field of experience). I've acquired supporters and donors simply from networking online. Networking doesn't have to be this awkward "I have to go do this" type of experience anymore. There are so many opportunities for those who are not social butterflies to network and connect with those who share similar interests and motivations.

Volunteering is another great way to network and may be easier for those who are introverts or intimidated by large crowds.

Taking a Breather

I've often been told by family members and colleagues that "you won't be any good to anyone else unless you take care of yourself." A big part of taking care of yourself mentally and emotionally is stepping away to take a breather. Sometimes we get so immersed in our dreams and aspirations that we fail to see them through objectively.

I've found that stepping away sometimes can help more than it can hinder you. For those highly driven folks like myself, it can be extremely hard to step away from the long 'to do' list or all the things you aspire to do on your imaginary timetable but stepping away is necessary. It can literally be stepping away from your desk, project or events for some time. This could also simply mean being "still" mentally so that God (your higher power) can help give you clarity. Sometimes opportunities can give us a false sense of purpose but it's not until you allow God to really direct your path, career and endeavors that you will see doors open. When you truly tap into what God has you here for you will see all of your branding, projects and dreams through a different lens.

Don't Allow Fear, Generational Strongholds or a Lack of Knowledge Keep You From Stepping Out Your Comfort Zone

Never let the facts that you haven't been 'groomed' for something frighten you from embarking on a new journey. I never saw myself as a business woman when I was younger. Now I'm a respected business woman who helps others develop their businesses. Simply do the work (research and due diligence) and stay a student.

I do not have a formal education in communications or marketing nor have I ever interned for a company doing so. I taught myself all that I know.

Take It Easy On Yourself

Recently someone told me that I needed to stop being so hard on myself. That, along with a LOT of affirmations about how 'I am enough' have collectively helped me better understand that I need to ease up on myself. One of the upsides of being surrounded by a lot of go-getters is that you never forget to keep striving for more or better. The downside is that you tend not to cut yourself any slack. We all want to be successful. Why are we so hard on ourselves though?

Why do we keep acting like whatever God has for us isn't going to manifest as long as we give 100% to what we do? Just like being unproductive and lazy won't work in your favor... neither does beating yourself up. Why? Because anytime you reach a goal or attain some type of achievement, there will be something else to attain. It sounds cliché but life is truly about the journey and you can't enjoy it constantly waiting for the next thing to happen without enjoying where you are. I was supposed to be a statistic... a pregnant illiterate teenager from Chicago who stayed on government assistance.

Despite all of the aforementioned, I'm healthy, in my right mind, I have my own business, I attended one of the top universities in the country (despite not testing well) and I've had the privilege of blessing others who started out like myself. Don't get hung up on your mistakes, the bad cards you're dealt, shortcomings and what you don't have. Just be thankful.

Your gifts are not about you. Leadership is not about you. Your purpose is not about you.

A life of significance is about serving those who need your gifts, your leadership, your purpose. – Kevin Hall, author *Aspire*

Ask Yourself If You Want To Be An Entrepreneur?

Determine if you truly want to be a full-time entrepreneur or if you have a gift that can be nurtured while continuing to work. When you are doing what you love and what God has called you to do so, your opportunities are limitless. If you desire to produce a product or provide a service that requires more time than you can provide while working you may have to determine what will work best for your family.

Entrepreneurship is a faith walk. Your passion is what will get you through those times you want to give up and get a 9 to 5.

Your passion will propel you into opportunities you may have never imagined. All of these opportunities will work together for the greater good of your business, brand and body of work. As opportunities become available you will get more clarity of your vision and how you can tweak what you're doing to reach the next level. The great part about LEGACY building is that it's ongoing and forever evolving.

Your brand is more than a business, a slogan or logo. You are your brand. The popularity of the term "brand" may come and go but your LEGACY is forever. Until then...Build. Build. Build.

6

From the Chaos of a Startup to the Calm from a Profit
Pierre DeBois

• • •

When Julie Holloway asked me to write a chapter for the third TEW book, I was truly honored - but also felt overwhelmed. A TEW chapter is meant to answer the question "Why did I start my own business?" It's an honest question, one that every entrepreneur faces, and I do get it often.

Yet despite being interviewed many times over the past 6 years, I have not thought about a chapter-length written answer until now. Analytics is a complicated, technical subject. Working in analytics is not as straightforward or an everyday choice as opening a restaurant or being a freelance website designer. My entrepreneurial choice came from a number of unique life chances and instances. I weigh carefully when giving advice or revealing a story – each word needs to help someone, and in life the value of what you hear varies by situation.

So I was uncertain if my TEW contribution would really help shape a business owner's judgment. But I was sure my response would help entrepreneurs feel less overwhelmed. So here's my story, told with a wish that what I share makes your choices better.

I started with analytics as an effort to support Lesco Logistics, a 1500-employee government contract firm started by my cousin Anita Williams. At the time – 2005 - Lesco was one of Alabama's largest minority-owned contracting firms. The firm wanted to verify how its website content was impacting its customer lifecycle, to best manage marketing costs and team resources. The answer came in adding web analytics to the website. I educated myself through analytics training at my expense and later worked with the firm's developer to deploy the analytic script on the site. I then realized the potential for analytics to connect with businesses at a critical moment; deploying a marketing strategy to generate sales.

Now analytics was not my first choice for a business idea to pursue. I had attended graduate business school to transition from being an automotive design engineer for 8 years to being a venture capitalist who could help minority businesses gain investment opportunities. I also worked through the AmeriCORP program at AccionUSA, a microlender for small businesses. Accion opened my eyes to what small businesses face in term of financing, particularly for those businesses started by women and people of color.

But I soon learned that most venture capital firms do not operate in markets in which many minority-owned businesses serve. The return on investment on those markets usually averages lower than a rate that VCs typically seeks. The good news since my graduate school days is that the number resources are increasing, thanks to Small Business Investment Companies (SBICs) dedicated to minority businesses, the rising number of crowd sourcing platforms, and new incubators, such as Blue1647, a tech incubator in Chicago, and NewMe Accelerator, a startup incubator in San Francisco.

I soon realized that I had to pivot my passion - helping small businesses while assisting larger firms – from a finance career solution (VC) to a marketing career solution (strategy and analytics). Doing so connected what I want to do with the industry's reality.

But I did not launch Zimana until 2009. I had left the contracting firm, and had moved to New York to join an advertising agency; concerned that analytics was not ready for small businesses as a market. But I did find data to prove what small businesses were spending on digital marketing, a trend that would prove useful in marketing analytics. I found it just in time – I was laid off 6 months after joining the ad agency. Having just turned 40 and reaching a year after my dad had passed away, I decided to pursue building Zimana, right from my Brooklyn apartment.

A few words on Zimana (ok, this book is written by business owners - you should have expected a small sales pitch!): Zimana is a web analytics consultancy that helps businesses improve their marketing through determining relevant results from their social media and analytics reports. An analysis typically includes drawing conclusions from web analytics data, such as visitor behavior analysis, marketing strategy ideas, and suggested adjustments for website content. Zimana clients encompass mom and pop businesses to large firms. Zimana is among the first minority-owned analytic services firms.

My purpose in this chapter is to focus on information that helps you, the reader, operate your business for the long haul. That kind of success is not guaranteed. The majority of businesses go under within 5 years for various reasons. A business thrives when it serves its customers well while playing to its strengths.

But there can be hindrances for a start-up owner to develop those business strengths, and I had a fair share. At the beginning I was unsure how exactly analytics services would work for small businesses. Educating small businesses on analytics consumed a lot of time - many owners still believe it is just SEO when it is much more – and spending too much time educating can slow operations and slow revenue. To address it, I refined my networking pitch to give a clear explanation of analytics' value while starting a dialogue that would answer questions. I also made sure that my website content complemented my pitch – no verbal pitch should be longer than a few sentences, so a website and social media should convey details that can answer a potential client's questions.

Experience gaps can hinder, too. When I started I did not fully understand website design elements. Yet knowing where to adjust HTML in a website was essential in explaining to customers how analytics tags work and bring value. So I trained on web development and made reading resources a high priority between client meetings. Great customers are educating themselves all the time. Business owners have to keep up.

One by product from reading and educating – I picked up interest from a number of digital marketing news sites to write on analytics. I currently write for CMS Wire, Solution Providers for Retail, and All Analytics. This freelance effort has provided some additional content marketing, an aspect many B2Bs continue to overlook.

The need to educate also addresses another hindrance: Minority owned businesses looking to overcome corporate spending biases, even in an era with the first African-American US president in office. Despite the touting of diversity on corporate fliers, subtle racism in business culture can undermine opportunities to be significantly visible. Moreover, subtle racism is extremely difficult to fight. Many times I faced subtle racism that could have limited my career choices. To circumvent those obstacles, I focused on achieving results that made bias questionable. A relentless focus on results will eventually put you around the right people who meaningfully want your contribution and avoid those who don't.

The drive for results is also helpful when working remote from clients, which is how Zimana has typically worked.

People are skeptical when starting projects without in-person communication. Earnestly, guiding customer expectations when communicating project statuses through a web conference or an email engenders trust from your client. Savvy clients who are comfortable with tech learn that communication with you online and offline is the same.

Finally when it comes to hindrances in business, there is nothing more derailing than continual chaos. Chaos in new businesses develops from working on activities that changes urgency almost hourly – a new client that was to start on Monday delays by a month, leaving you scrambling to replace revenue. A delivery problem crops up. A software crash eliminates records. Chaos ensues because one task can quickly trigger several more haphazardly, leaving no time to make strategic decisions.

To grow, businesses have to reduce chaos by developing systematic support such as online invoicing and customer service communication. Becoming systematic helps businesses highlight reoccurring costs and be more efficient at resolving efforts that are meaningful to serving customers better. Think of this as bringing the Pareto rule – 80% of your business results come from 20% of your business efforts – to life. Minimizing chaos lets you see that crucial connection - the difference between making arbitrary decisions and choosing that 20% that keeps your doors open.

Chaos can also arise from fraud conducted by bad partners, and sometimes, bad customers. Scrutinize your processes for onboarding customers and partners. Maintain email records that accurately reflect agreements and intentions. Reducing the chaos from fraud lets you refocus on the customers and partners who are ethical and make work fun.

Many entrepreneurs say they started businesses to follow their passion and leave their old job or career. That desire to be free appeals to everyone, with messages appearing in business-related media every day. But the irony is that to grow a business effectively, entrepreneurs must develop systematic protocols that mimic those in the corporate world – the very world they dream to escape. Those protocols minimize chaos, and have helped the best corporations survive economic downturns.

In many ways minimizing chaos allows you to increase your effort to deliver on customer expectations. You have to demonstrate how you accomplish your tasks for customers and partners the same way you do for your supervisor and managers. What you demonstrate is critical because every missed opportunity to demonstrate means less revenue in the bank. Customer requests can arrive anytime, thanks to the internet, and you must be timely in your results. There is never really a "time out" in running a business. Supportive resources will be scarce, and isolation will seem abundant. You are in a constant state of war - a battle to win customers and clients for the long haul.

So to prepare for that war, here are a few tips for building your business.

1. **Use cloud services that can speed transactions and increase convenience** – Cloud services are online software that makes operational tasks easy such as conferencing with remote partners, answering customer questions, and managing accounting affairs. They are cloud-based invoicing solutions, such as Paypal, Freshbooks, and Quickbooks, that expands customer payment options to include credit cards. These tools can also graph income and expenses for more concise spending decisions.

2. **Monitor influences in breakeven and profit margins** – Being relentless in managing expenditures over time will ultimately improve cash flow. Look for tools that can graph expenses over time. Cut reoccurring fees where possible. Reducing reoccurring fees is one way to decreased fixed costs and to improve profitability. Take the invoice solutions I mentioned in Point 1. Many charge a monthly fee, while a few charge only when there is a transaction. When business is slow, that transaction-only charge will occur less often, becoming one less fixed cost that can eat into earnings consistently.

3. **Use analytics to manage your marketing choices** – Many people still link analytics to search engine optimization (SEO), but understanding where your traffic is sourced can highlight great choices for paid search, social media, and other marketing tools. Don't focus for the right amount of data – instead use analytics to plan your website and social media so that your business can interact with customers in between the first meeting and the actual sale.

4. Budget your marketing time and money to pivot on digital media wisely – Many small businesses over-rely on one advertising medium to give customers a message. People are bombarded with messages – even more so as they access the internet through multiple devices - so their attention span is limited. Deploying social media and paid search plans, with an analytical eye for how customers access the internet, can help draw their attention consistently for your products, services, or events.

5. Beware of "hustling" multiple products and services without assessing market trends – Many people hear the phrase "hustling" and imagine that selling a lot of different items is good. But hustling really describes your effort behind a well thought-out product or service, not just a collection of stuff that you hope will sell. Look for studies that indicate marketplace trends then determine how that product or service solves a problem for a customer based on that trend. I delayed launching Zimana until I could find trends that indicated small businesses online spending matched the demand for website and marketing spending. Finding that trend made selling analytic services easier by showing hesitant leads that competitors were investing in analytics, too.

6. Defer purchases during the early years of operation – There can be a temptation to spend spontaneously when business is good. Consumers spend on a whim and want. Such spending in business creates cashflow problems. Instead, real business owners vet every dollar and reinvest earnings into tools that impact the customer experience. In bootstrapping the start of Zimana, I eliminated most personal entertainment, held back on replacing my car (14 years old as I write this), and avoided clothing purchases for 4 years to ensure that I did not spend on a purchase that would cut off a necessity later.

7. **Make sure your customers match an intended customer profile** – Develop an ideal customer persona so that your marketing can attract the right customers and partners. A defined persona also minimizes interactions with people and partnership requests that are not fit your services.

8. **Find ways to interact with people in a non-conditional way** – Because running a business engenders endless tasks, you can overdo requesting a task, favor, or barter, be it from friends or professional relationships. Do yourself a favor. Make time to do a small business owner, a friend, or family member a simple favor without requiring an exchange. In short, be human.

9. **When networking, look for people who can GSD - get stuff done** – Deal with people who follow-up promptly, can explain concerns logically, and can manage details to completion. Such people can make project complications easier to address, and are proactive in developing a solution. (Note that this skill is one expected in a corporate job – see what I mean about behavior that does not go away?)

While vetting people, make sure you can GSD, too. Sometimes people overemphasize networking over capability. Don't be one of those people! Manage your network so that your links and social media profiles do not imply misleading associations. Protect your credibility as you move forward.

10. **Use pictures and video to explain your benefits and features** – Customers relate to images of how your offering can benefit them, as well as behind-the-scene moments to learn who is behind the business. Use 40 or so pictures and videos to save editing time choosing media for social media sharing. Update your media periodically and keep generic "stock photos" to a minimum.

Finally, while eliminating chaos, measuring your results, and fighting for profitability, remember to enjoy the journey. When you look back, you should feel pride and the urge to grin from your accomplishments. Hopefully you'll have a few ideas and the urge to share a chapter-length written answer with other entrepreneurs.

7

Tips for Elevating, Success, Inspiration, Growth + Pushing Through
Tamika Maria Price

• • •

As an entrepreneur, I have learned through this journey that it takes more than just wanting to succeed. There are specific elements to raising the bar, moving toward greatness and preparing the appropriate foundation when even pondering being in business for yourself. Here are tips that I believe will encourage you and allow you much room for elevation, success, growth and inspiration building your empire as a small business owner. These tenants come from what I have learned through my experiences as an entrepreneur. I hope you are inspired and gain wisdom to move forward and push through.

Time Management – Are You Busy or Productive?
The word "busy" has been glamorized and too many confuse the word 'busy' for 'productive'. They may have slight relation, but in no way are the two

synonymous. You can call yourself 'busy' all day messing around on Facebook, answering emails, and ordering office supplies, but was that a 'productive' use of your day? It can happen to the best of us. We mean to log onto Facebook just for a few minutes and between scrolling your timeline, responding to the comments of your latest selfie and responding to the dozens of event invitations, it turns into an half hour!

I learned a great time management strategy from an event planner. She suggested at the "Spark and Hustle" women's conference to account for every minute of your day. She suggested using a desk or your cell phone's calendar to break down all of your tasks into allocated blocks of time. She instructed to allow all of your calls and emails to go unanswered until it was the time of day you allocated to respond to them. Most phone calls and emails we receive throughout the day are not time sensitive, but I was treating them as such. Think of this method as a "to-do" list on steroids. It kept me accountable and on task every minute of my work day. I made calls, wrote my book and even allocated time for social media. By breaking down my goals into smaller tasks, it allowed me to focus on everything while maintaining productivity.

You Are In Sales.
So many people hate the idea of and the word 'sales', but if you want to grow as an entrepreneur you absolutely have to get comfortable with selling. No matter what industry you are in, understand and accept that you are in sales. You are selling yourself, your products, your services and your brand. If you are a

one-man operation, your image has an even heavier weight in regards to whether a person will buy what you are selling. As a small business owner, the selling and buying process is on a much more personal level than your local "Walmart". They have strongly established themselves as the "low cost leader". You know you are not getting stellar service, but you know you are getting it at a low price. People know exactly what they are going to get when they shop at Walmart. As the entrepreneur, you need to take into careful consideration everything you wear, say and do on and off the clock including face-to-face and social media interactions. Ask yourself,

"Does this align with my goals?"

"Is this message positive?"

"Is this message clear, concise and useful?"

All too often, we let our fear of rejection overpower the fact that effective sales is all about helping find a solution to a problem and building a relationship with your customer (or potential customer). We get worried that we will hear "no" and guess what? You will definitely hear no's but you will not die – I promise.

Effective sales is ultimately about doing less talking and more listening. If you are scared of the word 'sales', then focus more on researching relationship building.

Think about it – how can you effectively offer solutions to a potential client if you do not know anything about them? Relationship-building is single-handedly the most important aspect of building your small business, no matter what industry you are in.

Create Multiple Streams of Income.
This is another phrase we hear a lot in the world of business, but I do not see enough of my fellow entrepreneurs actually doing it. Some of those I see doing it, are not doing it the right way. Unless you are a venture capitalist or a shark from the show "Shark Tank", you should not have your hands in multiple, unrelated businesses. That makes you appear untrustworthy and scatterbrained. We have all had the friend that is a Mary Kay rep in January, a realtor in April and a wedding planner by the holiday season. This type of 'grasshopper' entrepreneur is only making it harder because they have to continuously start over and their friends and family are tired of buying what they are selling.

To effectively create multiple streams of income, create complimentary product and service offerings. This is what I did, even having had two separate businesses, an annual charity fashion event and a non-profit organization. I began offering wardrobe styling and personal shopping services in November 2008. I did not know anyone in the industry and started off by invested in a polished, professional website and attending at least two networking events per week to market my services. I attended as many women's conferences as I could and networked my tail off. I was simultaneously planning the first *Dangerous Curves Ahead* charity fashion show, which turned into an annual event, now with its seventh installment. This charity event landed me my first television appearance on NBC 5 News and continues to build its following for its charitable component (making over moms in need) as well as having women of all shapes represented on the runway.

After working one-on-one with women on their everyday and professional wardrobe for just over six months, I was contacted by the "Racheal Ray Show" to do on-camera wardrobe makeovers. This national media coverage was huge in putting me on the map as a local wardrobe stylist/personal shopper. I began to focus more with speaking engagements and media outreach. I made it a point to build relationships with and pitch local media, resulting in being featured on the Chicagoland TV morning show, ''You & Me This Morning' and nationally on WGN News. Soon after, I realized I was lacking a product to sell at my speaking engagements and started to write my first book, Standout Style: The Shopping + Style Guide for Real Women, released in August of 2010. A book not only is another stream of income, but it lands you more media features and further solidifying your reputation as an expert in your field.

Fast forward to 2014, when my husband (my biggest supporter, business advisor and 'keep-it-real-with-me-even-if-it-hurts confidante) and I decided to further build the brand of Standout Style, with a brick and mortar, Standout Style Boutique was born. I want to be clear, honest and candid: opening a storefront is extremely risky and requires a significant investment (for us, over $20K to be exact and would have been more, without keen negotiation skills). Having a brick and mortar this past year has taught me so much. Although we had a detailed business plan, you can not anticipate anything until you are living it. You must have a plan B for your plan B and remove every drop of ego you thought you had if you want to be successful.

Every stream you create can be considered a risk if it takes significant time, effort and/or money to launch. This is why it is so important to carefully plan, research and strategize the short and long term goals for your brand and business(es) so you stay on track and make smart choices.

Seek Wise Counsel.
If you are truly seeking success as an entrepreneur, then you understand the value of and consistently seeking wise counsel. The key word in this phrase is 'Wise'. In most situations our friends and family should not be considered wise counsel, unless they are where you are trying to go career-wise. Understand that most family and friends will not understand your untraditional thinking and entrepreneurial spirit. They may call you crazy or try to talk you out of your business ideas and dreams because it does not make sense to them. Or you'll receive the, 'Why you just do not go and find a "good job" somewhere?' type responses. If you have already shared your ideas with them and were met with anything other than constructive criticism, love and support, learn to keep that part of your life to yourself, at least at the beginning.

One of the most successful women in business right now, Sara Blakely of Spanx, the uber successful line of shapewear, said it best: *"Ideas are most vulnerable in their infancy. Family and friends often express concern or doubts (out of love) that can stop people dead in their tracks. Share once you've invested enough of yourself in it, to the point when you know there is no turning back. If you share too soon, ego has to get involved and you will spend more time explaining and defending your idea rather than pursuing it. But definitely tell the people that can help move your idea forward."*

Those who can help you move your idea forward are wise counsel. They along with your vision will be the connection to your dreams coming to fruition.

8

Outliving the Circumstances
Pray, Prepare and Perform
Renee Jefferson Smith

• • •

I have faced so many challenges in life that a person walking in my shoes would not have made it down the block. Okay, not too many horrible challenges but surely ones that could have been prevented. Only if someone would have told me that getting married at 18 and passing up eighteen scholarships was not the thing to do. That was the moment that I thought I had all the answers and was afraid to listen to that voice of wisdom that would help make things a lot easier. After over twenty years of searching for the answers, I finally understand my purpose in life. Not all things are clear, but I know for sure that I have been placed here to help others. Nothing that I do is solely about me, but more so for the betterment of those around me. Many times we walk around praying for the answers, hoping that a person will speak life into our situation, but in most cases God has already given you the answer and is just waiting on you to MOVE.

The Power of Prayer

There were times in my life that I had no clue where I was going and how I was going to get there. I knew that God created me for success, but it was just about learning how to obtain it. My mind was sometimes like a shooting star. Day in and day out I would come up with a new business idea and I was for sure that it would help me to become the millionaire that I dreamed of being. I would often calculate my profits before establishing the product. One day while riding in my car I started thinking about all that I had going on, all the projects that were incomplete and everything that was falling behind as a result of me being overwhelmed. I immediately started to pray. Through the power of prayer I was able to speak clarity over my purpose, identify my true passions and purpose and find comfort in knowing that although I'm great at most things, God has designed me for a specific area in life. From that day forward I learned to pray about everything. I spoke daily over my home, my children and my business. I prayed over my finances, my future and my faith. Often we doubt ourselves and it was important for me to be reminded that I was not only capable of more but I was created for GREATNESS.

"Lord, thank you for your daily insight into my life. I know that I was made for greatness and I thank you for helping to identify my true purpose here on earth. I ask you to guide my mind so that I make decisions that are pleasing to you. I thank you for wisdom and insight over all that concerns me. I thank you that daily I remain healthy and no weapon formed against me shall

prosper. I speak increase over my financial affairs. I thank you in advance that my bank accounts are full and that my life is full of joy. I thank you in advance for sending individuals my way that will bring positive influences to all that concerns me. I thank you that you are placing me on a path to my destiny, for you know my dreams, my thoughts and my deepest feelings. With you all things are possible and I know I'm on my way to my wealthy place."

I have learned that the power of prayer changes everything. It puts everything into perspective and daily you start to understand your why. Why you go through what you've gone through, why the desire is burning so deep to succeed and why you are reading this book.

The Process of Planning

In life we often find ourselves making excuses for almost everything. Most people go through life with no plans for their day, their week and not even close to planning for their future. Planning is very important. When starting my journey as a business owner I have learned to plan years in advance. Developing of a plan helps you to achieve the goal. Now please understand that setting a goal and developing a plan are two different things. You can have a goal to go back to school to obtain your degree but if you never visit the school or complete the application then in reality you really don't have a plan. When you plan for your future God provides you clarity so that you can see past the circumstances that may arise in the process. I can remember God giving me clarity about my true purpose. He set before me a project that would cost more than what all my bank accounts total together. Just when I started to lose faith and make up excuses, God reminded me not to worry about the when, where, who or how. I was given an assignment and it was time for me to start planning. So although you may not have all the tools that you need to obtain your dream, you should always start planning.

Steps to planning

1. Invest in a journal
Journaling is so important. It is imperative that you write down your thoughts, your feelings and your goals. This will allow you to stay on track and keep moving forward towards what God has planned for you.

2. Do your research
Make sure that you understand what it is that you are tackling. It is good to know the ends and out of your journey, and although you may come across some stumbling blocks, you will learn a lot as you go. Be prepared to meet many people, ask lots of questions and make many sacrifices.

3. Create a budget
This is sometimes the hardest thing for individuals to focus on. We always know that we want to start a business, purchase a home, a new car or even save, but we never really understand how to create a budget or what it will truly take for us to accomplish our goals. By having a budget it will allow you to know what you are working with and just how far you can get with achieving your goal.

4. Ask questions

Don't ever be afraid to ask questions. When doing your research identify people that are currently practicing in a similar field. Perhaps they have already purchased a home or accomplished a huge goal. God has already ordered your steps, and surely your journey may not be someone else's but understand while on this path to fulfillment he will place people in your path to help you along the way.

5. Build relationships with the right individuals

Build relationships with all the right people. You will meet many people, some good and bad. Please know that everyone that you will meet will not always support you, they will not be your friend, and yes they will talk about you and eyeball your vision. However you will meet many people that will fall in love with your dreams, pray for you when you're sleeping, invest into your brand and encourage you through the entire process.

6. Never give up

Through all of these steps the most important one is to never give up! Unfortunately life is one of those things that doesn't come with instructions. For most things we know how to put together but we are never truly told how to handle the challenges. When problems arise, continue to press on. When friends disappear, continue to press on. Even when you are tired and can't see the way, continue to press on. One thing that I have learned about life, before anyone else can believe in you, you first have to believe in yourself. No matter what the storm looks like, NEVER GIVE UP!

The Act of Performing

I must admit there are times when I get lazy. There are times when I just don't feel like moving forward. I get tired from the constant job of motherhood, being business owner and even the daily routines that come with living. We are consumed with bills, problems, responsibilities and even heartache. There will always be those times when we just want to give up. As we all know, giving up is not an option. Through sacrifices, perseverance and determination I learned to never ever give up. When you realize that you cannot fail, you also understand that the only thing left to do is to perform. That means to give it all you got! Yes, it may take all that you have, but you have to get busy. You can no longer lie around dreaming, wishing and hoping about your dream; you now have to go after it.

Realize that no one is going to do it for you, so this accomplishment will all be a part of your efforts. Through this process you are never alone. God is always and will always be by your side. That's the one thing that kept me grounded, is knowing that he was there every step of the way. As the old saying goes, when the going gets tough, the tough gets going. You are tough and made from the very best. You were made to conquer, built to last and you are filled with all the tools that you need to help you achieve your vision.

Your circumstances don't have control over you; however you have control over them. So if you are a single mother, a victim of abuse, recently lost your job or perhaps your dreams are blurry, God already created the vision, the purpose and the plan. Now it's time for you to get focused, get moving and live the life that you one day dream that you'll have.

9

Delayed is not Denied
LaTasha West

You miss 100% of the shots that you don't take.
- Wayne Gretzky

• • •

You can also miss 100% of the shots that you do take. That's an important lesson that many entrepreneurs, wantraprenuers and wouldbepreneurs need to learn.

The road less traveled is not easy and most often will be full of wrong turns, obstacles and roadblocks. This is a very, very uncertain journey and those brave ones who take the leap must be prepared for the only certainty which is UNCERTAINTY.

One must have a spirit of resilience, a will to win and the strength to fight! Understand that the ride is wild and bruises are a part of the ride. The best idea may fail, your well executed plans may go unseen, but you must keep going if your goal is to win.

Speaking of winning....all entrepreneurs need to learn early on how to define winning for themselves. You cannot judge yourself by someone else's definition of success. If you don't know what success looks like for you, STOP READING THIS RIGHT NOW! Take a few minutes and write down what you want, be clear and detailed. Not what the world says is success, but what will make YOU happy. Once you know this you can proceed.

I've been there done that. I've quit a job that I hated and started a business that I hated. Sounds insane right? It is! That was me letting the world define success for me. When I got clear on what worked for me, I began to make major shifts. I like to call this my #PIVOT. Oh and by the way I've had many pivots and I presume that you will also. It's okay! Trust me, get the lesson and keep moving.

I believe that I was born an entrepreneur, not that I knew what that word meant then. I just knew I wanted to run things and make money.

Ask anyone who knows me and they will say I'm a hustler. I've been hustling for as long as I can remember. My first memory of wanting my own business and my own money was when I was about 7 or 8 years old. I was staying at my grandparent's house in the summer and I overheard my grandfather mention that there were too many dandelions in the yard. Something stirred within me; I saw an opportunity to make some money. This was at that point that I brokered my first deal! I persuaded my grandfather to allow me to pull up the dandelions at a cost of $.05 per dandelion. That day I got a taste of making deals and making money, I was hooked after that.

That was the first of many opportunities that I created for myself, some of them have not gone quite as well. Being an entrepreneur involves a low level of foolishness, you must be willing to take chances and sometimes risk it all without the guarantee of a positive return. I have definitely been a fool in business before.

I recall having this great idea to open a clothing boutique, I figured, *Hey, people always compliment me on what I am wearing, so naturally they will buy from me.* That was pretty much all of the thought I put into it. The next day I was up and at it, I convinced the salon owner where I got my hair done to let me rent the front of her salon. I went online found places to order clothes wholesale, located a local place where I could buy women's accessories at a wholesale rate and viola' I had a boutique. Within 30 days of my bright idea my store was open, awesome right? WRONG! I failed to mention that I had a full time job at the time, so I couldn't reasonably run a boutique. Dilemma number 1: now I needed to hire someone. Where would I find someone? I didn't have any money to pay an employee. What hours will the boutique be open?

Well, by the goodness of my creator I found someone willing to work the hours that I needed, for what I could afford to pay. Great right? Wrong again! The person I hired had absolutely no sales experience, did not know how to set up/close down a store (neither did I) and they did not dress or present them self in the way I wanted my boutique's image to reflect. Deep sigh. I figured I could work around this; I just need a body in the space. *The items would sell themselves considering the patrons of the salon had to walk through the boutique to get to the salon area.* You guessed it- WRONG again! Not only did the items not sell themselves, they actually grew legs and started walking out of the boutique! My employee did not give a darn about my inventory, therefore they weren't monitoring it. When I came to the store to check inventory, many items were missing and there was no cash in exchange for them.

You can imagine my frustration at this point. Even though there was no cash for the inventory missing, the rent still needed to be paid, the employee still needed to be paid for their time AND I needed to buy more inventory. Where would this money come from? It came from my weekly paycheck. My husband was not too happy about that little detail. I ended up letting the employee go and hiring another, who was better at sales, but this person needed to bring their child to work with them. (I can't make this up). Being the inexperienced business person, I agreed to this. I'm sure I do not need to tell you this situation did not end well.

As you can probably guess, I closed the boutique and took a loss. However any true business person knows there is a lesson in everything. From this experience and a few other not so successful endeavors, I learned not to move so quickly. I learned that planning even in its most minor form is needed. I learned how to create a job description and candidate profile. I learned the meaning of location, location, location. I learned that it takes a heck of a lot more to run a store than to buy some things to sell and slapping up an open sign! Along with the many lessons learned I walked away with some pretty nice clothes that never sold! But hey a girl can never have too many pieces of clothing.

The boutique taught many things. Some of the lessons that I took away were:

1. I needed a plan
2. I did not want a business with a high overhead (rent, inventory, displays etc.)
3. If I was going to hire workers, they should be qualified for the job
4. I needed to know how to run the business that I planned to open or I needed to hire someone who did
5. I needed the time to work my business
6. I might want to do some marketing or advertising so that people know I am here

When I launched my next business (you didn't think I gave up did you?) I was able to use the lessons learned to map a plan to create a successful business. In 2011, I left my corporate job and jumped in with both feet. I launched my virtual assistant business providing administrative support for other small businesses. In this business I have the pleasure of assisting other new and struggling business owners to avoid making some of the same mistakes that I did. At the time of this publication I am preparing to launch yet another business which builds upon the skills that I have acquired on my entrepreneurial journey.

As I warned you at the beginning the journey is not easy, it will be full of bumps, bruises and tears. It'll be worth it once you get there. Remember DELAYED DOES NOT

MEAN DENIED, if you do not succeed at first, get the lesson and keep moving ahead.

Wishing you all the best!

10

The Birth of Windy City Mix
Rodrigo Alvear

• • •

Some of the greatest moments of my life, in one way or another, involve laughter. Just the sound of hearing a friend, a client, or child laugh can cause me to pause and reflect on how that same sound changed the course of my life. In my career as a DJ, I have made it my passion to listen to subtleties that are often masked by music. A song played during a father-daughter dance may sound nice to a crowd of invited guests, but that same song means something else entirely to a father seeing his little girl all grown up. The sound of silverware gently hitting a glass creates the ever-so-popular tradition of asking a bride and groom to kiss, but that sound can represent something different to a DJ who has heard it time and again.

But of all the noises and sounds I've heard throughout my life, none has made such an impact as that of laughter - possibly the most rewarding response to a comment one can make. By that same token, the same sound is possibly the most disheartening I've ever heard, and it occurred after I asked a close family member for support. At the time I did not understand the full impact of what his response meant to me, and in looking back at that exact moment I have come to accept and even appreciate that feeling of absolute humiliation.

Some of the greatest memories I have of my upbringing in Chicago revolve around the sheer joy that was made possible only through the power of music. You see, Latino homes, by their very nature, are loud places that have a particular frequency or soundtrack that stays with us throughout our lives. On our birthdays our parents would play a song we know ever-so-well as the *Mañanitas* song, and our version of *Happy Birthday To You* oftentimes included a green frog. I remember how loud family get-togethers were, and how there was no better noise than the opening of presents at the stroke of midnight on Christmas morning. I recall the sounds of the countless number of meals we shared, the sound of my brother and I arguing over something that seemed so important at the time, and the sound of my sister crying when I unintentionally made her young life unbearable.

I recall these sounds not only because the snap of a snare drum is eerily similar to the sound of a *chancla* hitting skin, nor because the echoes of a pipe organ remind me of some of the best parties of my youth, but rather because I discovered at an early age that there is a subliminal soundtrack which embodies our souls and becomes the tune by which we walk our path in life. Though I did not know this at the time, I devoted the years that followed to learning to hear that subtle sound, to capturing it then using it to create an impression so grand that it makes dance floors shake and walls tremble.

The story of my soundtrack, however, begins sometime around the age of 13. In retrospect, it seems that DJing was pretty much just put in my path as a young kid in 8th grade. If for no other reason, my mother decided it would be best to give her young son a gift that would keep him occupied and quiet for a few hours and which could possibly lead to a hobby. But in 1992, I did not really care too much for it. Come to think of it, how many 13-year-olds from back then thought about their path in life when Kris Kross and Sir Mix-a-Lot were playing on the stereo? My guess is very few.

At first, "playing" with turntables and being a DJ was nothing more than an activity that I was able to do at home. From there, it evolved into an opportunity to provide music for a family get-together, where I learned to blend sounds and listen to beats and queues from certain songs. More importantly, I learned that music had a cause-and-effect principal, and the better I made it sound, the more people I was able to get on the dance floor. I learned, by method of trial and error, what caused people to "feel" the sound. I taught myself how to match what I heard with what I saw, and I quickly learned to love the power that a true entertainer has over a cheering crowd. Still, though I spent much of my teen years studying the craft of DJing, it never occurred to me that it would be anything other than a hobby, where I was possibly able to get the attention of girls my age and possibly even make a few extra dollars on a part-time basis, but nothing more. Decades later I can reflect on this time period and smile at how naïve I was about that turntable and how it would change my life.

As I grew older, though, I learned that life does not always care about we want. By the end of 1998, the Bulls were no longer on another championship run, and I was booking a few DJ gigs here and there. Out of what was perhaps a mix of traumatizing childhood experience and the ego of recent Elmwood Park High School graduate, I created the stage name of "DJ Scarface" and quickly developed a good reputation for getting people on the dance floor. Still, I never imagined being able to make a living from working as a DJ, so I took a few classes at a local community college and found paying opportunities along the way. When we are young, though we think we are prepared and deserving of ruling the world, the reality is that we are able and willing to take odd jobs such as cleaning garbage at a warehouse, or package handling at UPS, or sorting endless amount of mail for the United States Postal Service, or even so much as becoming an Officer for the Cook County Sherriff's department. One opportunity lead to the next, but then came a point where I hit a wall and just didn't know what to do.

For those familiar with the reference, this was the "blue-pill, red-pill" point of my life.

There is nothing more belittling that being in a large financial bind and having absolutely no way of getting out of it. If necessity is the mother of invention, then certainly humility is the mother of desperation, and I learned this the hard way. I had no resources, no one to ask for help, and had no collateral or equity to turn into fast cash. I felt as though I was at the lowest point of my life, where I had to stand on something taller than I for a chance to reach up and touch rock bottom. So I turned to the one thing that I carried with me – I turned to that small hobby and prayed that DJ Scarface would provide a quick bailout for me and my family, and so I took the fastest and easiest method I knew how. To my surprise, I was able to get myself out of my situation by simply dedicating more time to my passion and finding small opportunities wherever they existed. What I could not predict was the next chapter of my life: how I was going to be presented with a chance to produce something that would change the course of my future.

The absolute greatest shock of my career was undoubtedly the first time I was paid for a high-profile event. My mind could not fathom someone paying me $750 to DJ a wedding. It was either too good to be true, or a cruel joke meant to attach my psyche just when I was on the verge of bettering myself. After controlling myself, getting the beating in my chest to subside to normal levels, and finally feeling air in my lungs again, I realized that I was on to something great. The $50 to $100 per gig that I was accustomed to was not ideal, but it was enough to keep a roof over my head and food on the table for my young family. I knew that going to work for another mindless boss at a meaningless company was not going to give me what I wanted in life; it was now or never for developing my own path. I had the confidence I needed. I had become an expert of my craft. I was a master of my form of art. I had no equipment. I owned none of the necessary tools in needed in order to become profitable, so I turned to those that I felt would understand my logic.

To this day I can still hear the sound of laughter that came forth from a certain individual upon my asking him for help. For artists of any kind, perhaps the greatest challenge they will face in their lifetimes (more so than financial) is finding someone to support them. I was still willing to take odd jobs here and there to pay bills, but I knew that I wanted to blaze a trail of my own. I confided on one person in particular, explaining everything I knew about how I could turn my passion into a business and how profitable the business would be. More than I had at any point in my educational career, I researched everything I needed to know about building a profitable business in the $8 Billion dollar wedding industry. The future of everything I envisioned for myself, my children, and for everything I held dear came down to one business meeting, which ended with the reverberating sound of laughter after I heard the words, "What?! A DJ business? Are you kidding me?". Though I had made it my life's ambition to work in an environment where noise and sound were constantly around me, never had I felt such deafening and defeating silence as I did at that moment.

Still, though my ego was bruised and battered, the dream was alive and well. I used what I had learned, including my past successes and failures, and used the negativity of others to fuel my fire for forging ahead. I envisioned a company of my own, and during a particularly long lunch hour I created a pipe-dream of an idea. At the time, the company I was working for informed me that my position was going to be eliminated in two weeks, so that's when I told myself that I was going to take the simple DJ dream to a legit, insured, professional company. I held a fun competition with friends at work, asking everyone to give me ideas on names for a fun and cool company that would provide high end DJs for all types of events with an emphasis on weddings (the winner would get a free party when i was established). Though most would be worried in knowing that, in less than two weeks, the idea of having a semi-steady paycheck would soon be gone, I was absolutely thrilled when at the end of that lunch hour we all came to an agreement with the name of "Windy City Mix". That 13-year-old boy who invested years of life in following an unpaved path now, finally, had a name for the soundtrack he was slowly producing.

After I decided to start the business with all the legal paperwork (and please believe me when I say it was no simple task), I began working from the basement of my apartment. I spent countless hours studying business strategies, getting tips and advice from vendors, salesmen, motivational speakers, books, and other DJ's. I developed a "whatever it takes" mentality, which provided the drive I needed to spend many sleepless, caffeine-fueled nights in front of a computer. I taught myself to design and build a website, though I had no one to visit WindyCityMix.com. I taught myself proper presentation etiquette and how to communicate effectively, though I did not have the ways or means of reaching potential customers. I had no office or place of business to call my own, so I met with clients at the local Panera or Starbucks. I was more determined than ever, and I knew that all I needed was the opportunity from a young couple to produce a wedding they and their guests would never forget, then for them to tell others about what I had done. Well, that opportunity happened....I was given "that one shot", and I have not looked back since.

No one, myself included, would have ever believed that Windy City Mix would be a profitable business, to the tune of over $100,000, with me at the helm along with some of the best DJ's in Chicago. I look back and I remember that first wedding and think of it as a stepping stone for what followed. All it took was a few good reviews and then the snowball effect took over. Before I knew it, I was getting booked for more than just weddings, but other high-scale events, and not just by friends and family. I walked in to locations where I would otherwise be unwelcome, and walked out as the hero who made a night a lasting memory. Before long, I was getting booked for months at a time, for parties more than a year away, and earning an income to support both my business and my growing family. When I started to get booked for multiple events for single dates, I panicked because I did not know what to do. Though I was overwhelmed by the amount of work, I certainly could not turn down the blessing of being able to make a living in doing what I loved, so I hired my very first employee. I hired a DJ, who was as passionate as I and was trained under my guidance, and the result created even more work for the two of us. With a greater workload, we hired, trained and established a bigger family of DJ's, and business continued to grow.

Though it took some years, I was able to find a small office where I could potentially host meetings and bring clients in to see how far we've come because of the hard work that I, along with a few mentors and friends along the way, was not afraid to take on. I learned to delegate my work, which is far easier said than done, and even hired a front desk receptionist to help talk to clients when I am unable to do so.

Though Windy City Mix has and will continue to flourish, it has not been without a great deal of hardships, sacrifices, and personal struggles. I am so proud to say that I built this business literally from the ground up, but I will not say that it has not cost me dearly in other ways. Though I hate to admit it, there was a time I did want to throw in the towel and just end what took me so long to create. It was in late 2013, early 2014. Though I had read and studied more about how to manage and maintain my business than ever, I failed to pay attention to other factors occurring at the same time. I unintentionally hurt those I loved, gambled with my own health and safety, and was creating a dark path along the busy road I helped establish.

I learned that rock bottom is possible even at the pinnacle of success, and though I was thriving in one aspect of life, I was crashing in another. I was really down and was ready to close the office doors - a lifetime of work was on the brink of collapse. I sought advice from other professionals in my industry and was very comforted to learn that we will all – at one point or another – hit that proverbial wall that will challenge us in ways we never thought possible. We will always fall but what matters is that we get back up and how we get back up. It took every last instinct in my being to not do it, and today I proudly say I am glad I kept the doors open; I did not give up or give in, and now a second set of office doors is soon to open as this company continues to grow.

In the beginning I never envisioned my company where it is today. I was just focused on being a DJ, and then on Windy City Mix being a DJ company with multiple DJs servicing all type of events. But in thinking about what we have accomplished, I look back with awe and I thank God for giving me the strength, knowledge, and patience to be where I am now. In all honesty, "I" am only one part of what "we" at Windy City Mix have established. While I did build this business from the ground up, it would have never happened with the support of a few good DJs and few good friends who have sat in my office for hours on end, brainstorming ideas and ways to grow.

Still, though I have so much to be grateful for, there are times when negativity creeps its way into our mix. As hard as I may try, I am not resilient to things that happen beyond my control. I am not more gifted, deserving, or talented than anyone else, but I am different from those that have not yet achieved their dreams because I refuse to let my passion go to waste. I learned to do whatever it takes - conduct my own research from different sources and come up with my own conclusions, draft my own ideas, my own pricing, my own marketing, build my team, etc. – to do what is best for me and for those that care about me and this dream of mine, and though I may stumble from time to time I will never do anything less than my absolute best for my team or my clients.

What began as a little push nearly 25 years ago has enabled me to be on the forefront of prosperity. If my awesome mother had not seen something in me and would have never bought me a set of turntables back in 1992, I definitely would not be the man I am – not just financially, but in every sense of the word. The lesson that I am learning today is that greatness does not rest on accomplishments of the individual, but rather what that individual can do to inspire greatness in others. I may not be the best example, but if for no other reason I know I can at least teach those that are working on achievements of their own. I find joy in talking to others, in meeting with other people that want to live their dream of having their own business. I try to show them my story of a simple little street DJ who turned it into his own little empire, and that with lots of faith, prayer, determination and the strength, it can definitely happen.

I do what I do because I absolutely love it. I have no other answer. I love what I do. I love working with my clients and will go well above and beyond to ensure their day is cherished long after my involvement is done. My greatest fear is letting down someone who counts on me – who relies on me to do what I do best – and I pray that I never get to the point where any client of mine gets less than they deserve. Windy City Mix has made it this far because I refuse to forget about the little clients who made this all possible. Opportunities have come and gone over the course of two decades, but while some doors have closed and opened, I have always wondered what would happen if I just simply knock those doors down and keep moving forward. I guess it's safe to say that it has worked out well thus far.

As for the soundtrack of my life…well, I don't know if I will ever finish the mix. I think it would be impossible to compress a lifetime of audio to one song or even an album, and frankly, I hope it never ends. I hope my soundtrack lives on, surpasses my life, and becomes a dance beat for my children, their children, and for anyone who is willing to listen to their passion. Success absolutely stems from a clear, unquestionable vision of greatness. Sometimes, however, the dreamer remembers the music before seeing the goal become reality. I'm just the man who heard the music, mixed it to a beat, and blasted it for the world to hear.

11

Learn How to Succeed in Any Circumstance
Dr. Toi Dennis

• • •

In life you operate from two places; in fear and in love. In your quest to fulfill your destiny, you must be willing to take risks. You must learn how to succeed in any circumstance. In my quest to pursue my passion I had to step out on faith and do it in fear and learn how to succeed in any circumstance.

As a young girl growing up my family faced many challenges. My mother was a single parent raising four children struggling to meet our basic needs at times and dealing with her own personal issues. There were many times where we didn't have a place to live and became homeless. As the oldest of four and the only girl often I found myself being in the mother role. That involved learning how to take care of myself and my siblings while trying to succeed in any circumstance.

I thank God for the many blessing that he put upon my family because our situation could have been worst. The people that he placed in my life throughout high school inspired me to want to make a difference. The community helpers, resources and case workers that instilled hope back into my family not only inspired me they challenged me with an educational opportunity. I was allowed to take a college a course my senior year in high school and if I did well in it I could attend the community college once I graduated. My experience was successful and from that point life changed forever.

I was no longer that lost little girl that was only taught to get your high school diploma and find a job. All the bad grades I received in high school didn't make me a bad person and keep me from making something of myself. My self-esteem and outlook on life was at the all-time highest. I could do anything I wanted to because after being in college for 12 years and receiving four degrees I finally had to stop hiding behind the books and start walking in my purpose.

Do It In Fear

Throughout my doctoral experience my topic was homelessness. I often reflected back to things I experienced growing up and how it made me feel. I wanted to do more research and learn more about how other children coped with being without a place to live and often no food to eat. I wanted to share with the world what I learned and bring awareness to the needs that are not being met in most of our communities.

I wrote my dissertation on homelessness and how it affects children's mental and behavioral health. Through my research experience I often thought about what I was going to do with this data that I collected and how I can make a difference in my community and society in general. After graduating with my doctorate in 2010, I started doing more research on the different areas that interested me the most and took notes on what resources were available for homeless women and children. I realized that there were not enough resources for women and children in the city and state that I had recently relocated to Clarksville, TN.

I started learning that there were more resources for men in the area than there were for women and immediately I want to do something about it. I wanted to start a transitional homeless shelter specifically for women and children. However, in my mind the spirit of defeat took over. How was I going to do this? Where was I going to get the money to start a business? I didn't know anyone except the professor that I met when taking a job at the local university. My ultimate question was how was I going to do this and be successful?

I was already feeling defeated before I even got started. I was worried about how people were going to receive my idea and me. I had everything down in my head but not on paper. Then one day I heard God say, *It's going to be okay.* You don't have to worry because you are doing what I called you to do, which is helping others and giving back to your community by providing women and children a place to stay. It would be a homeless shelter for women and children where I would provide a place of peace. In December 2012 Serenity House Women's Shelter Inc. was formed and our slogan became "Providing a Place of Peace."

My biggest supporter has been my husband of ten years. He helped guide me in the direction of getting my name branded and starting the paper work for the business. That was the easy part then I had to learn how to put my ideas down on paper. I was being asked questions from other business owners that I had never thought about. I was confident that I wanted to start a homeless shelter and help women and children. All that fear that I had in the beginning was starting to fade away because I was believing and trusting in God that this vision he gave me was going to be successful. Although, I still had a lot to learn I was willing to go through the process to take on the challenge.

The Process

There are many times where I found myself questioning if I was making the right decisions while I was trying to build my business plan, design programs and really making sure I was meeting the needs of the women in my community. I was in search of rare qualities so that my program wouldn't be the same as any other program in the area. I was striving for uniqueness and sustainability. I want to be able to offer wrap around services to women and children by allowing them to gain self-confidence and learn how to function successfully in our community. In doing all of this I must learn how form a team of individuals that believe in my vision, my goals and my overall mission. This team of individuals would be my Board of Directors.

How to Succeed in Any Circumstance

It took some time for me to realize that through the process and building my business there were going to be some ups and downs. People were going to come and go when you needed them the most and sometimes those people want to connect to you for the wrong reasons. You must know your circle and whom you are working with when starting a grass roots organization. Your team must be a working a team. Although, they may not work exactly like you when it comes to getting a task done; they still must have the drive and believe in your vision. You must know how to succeed in any circumstance because things can change in an instance.

Interacting Successfully
You don't have any control over most of the circumstances that you might encounter in life, but you do have the power to choose how you respond to those circumstances. Instead of worry about what the outcome of what may happen if there is a shift in your plans, choose to trust God and follow is his guidance come what may. There are going to be times when things will change within your business and how you handle those changes are important.

Be Optimistic
The difference between opportunities and obstacles is your overall outlook. Make sure you choose your reality over fantasy, not denying what's happening in the situation but instead choosing how you interact within your circumstances. Stay informed and choose to focus on the good instead of the bad. Allow God to inspire you through whatever experiences you go through by giving you a fresh perspective on them. Sometimes, you just have to sit back, take a deep breath and regroup.

Never Stop Learning

The more you take advantage of the constant stream of learning opportunities that God brings your way, the more success you will enjoy. Learn to evaluate the information that you encounter each day and apply it to the work that you are doing. We learn something from everyone that we meet whether it is a good or bad lesson. Evaluate how relevant the information is to you and how well it fits your life and overall needs for what you are trying to get done.

Keep Producing Value

In everything that you do, you want to consistently create value in what you are producing. Find creative ways to continue to meet the needs of your target population while drawing from the uniqueness that you bring. Adapting and keeping up the changes around you is vital to your overall success. Our society and their needs change rapidly.

Build Reserves

Prepare yourself to succeed during crises and other challenging circumstances by building relationships with change agents that you can draw on their support. Building partnerships with other community agencies and individuals that will help you build your brand even further. Continue to form a relationship with God so you can experience the peace he gives.

Embrace Discipline

In all that you do make time to consistently act on your intentions. Your priorities must be in place in order to be successful. Eliminate bad habits that waste your time and energy. Modify your activities so that you're not focusing on what matters the most.

The following tips are just a few ways to learn how to successfully succeed in your business and your personal life. Look at God! He has brought you this far and given you a vision that has changed your life and those around you because you are walking in your purpose. Embracing the challenges and adversities that life brings. Only you are responsible for your future. You only have one life to live, live it on purpose learn how to do it in fear and in love.

12

Love All and Happiness
Kasia Wereszczynska, M.A., LCPC, RYT

• • •

For years, I have been told by others how special I am.... I never knew what it really meant until most recently, when I discovered that my ability to multi-task, inspire peace and hope is priceless! There is something special about working in my field that highlights my strength about being brave...

Many times I'm asked the question, "Kasia, when did you decide to become an entrepreneur?" That question always makes me smile because I really never made the decision to become an entrepreneur--I was just thrown into the role. When you look up the definition of entrepreneur you see that it says, *someone who takes risks.* Well, I have been taking risks my entire life. The way I see it, the only way to be an effective entrepreneur is by taking risks. The world is a dynamic place. People, places, and things are constantly changing, and we need to change with them. Whether one is starting a business, developing a product, offering a service, leading a non-for-profit, or anything else, risk is always involved. Without risk there cannot be forward progress because we would all continue doing what is comfortable--a surefire means toward complacency.

Successful entrepreneurship requires a healthy mix of personality, experience, talent, skill, insight, and--of course--tons of motivation. What I have found is that a combination of what I have done throughout my life has manifested itself in everything I do today. I see myself as having been an entrepreneur since childhood. At age five my parents moved us from Poland to America. Like many other immigrant families, we had to literally reestablish ourselves from the ground up. I remember how hard my parents worked. They always had multiple jobs and always made sure that we were taken care of. Though I missed them often, I understood that they were doing everything they could to give us all the best lives possible. Just seeing their work ethic instilled something powerful inside me that keep me going to this day. They also helped me recognize the importance of celebrating diversity. To this point, I never forget my roots.

All of my experiences growing up, my education and my early adult life gave me the skills and provided the path that led me to becoming a successful entrepreneur. The day that I turned fifteen I earned a worker's permit and had three part-time jobs. Yes, that's right...three part-time jobs at age fifteen. Most people look at me like I'm crazy when I say that, but I swear it's the truth. Not only is it true, I loved it! I learned how to manage my time, prioritize tasks and I learned how to live an organized and disciplined life.

I always knew that I wanted to be in the position of saving lives. So, I immediately earned my CPR training and became a lifeguard. Simultaneously, I worked at a bakery and that was my start at developing strong communication and listening skills. I learned how to adapt my conversations to each customer and their needs. Through other part-time jobs I was able to tap into my creativity and learned I have a passion for creating new ideas to help and inspire others.

Outside of work I was also involved in swim team and ice skating. After all, I needed to show some school spirit and nurture my physical body and mind. This gave me the opportunity to learn about team work and provided a means to learn the feeling of belonging to a group and working towards a common goal. It taught how hard work and discipline pay off. In addition, I started my philanthropic journey by volunteering at a nursing home. Though my work there was oftentimes difficult, it was extremely rewarding. What I came to find here was that I had a gift with conversation. I could make the seniors smile, laugh, cry, reflect, and just about anything else I wanted and they needed.

I graduated from the Illinois School of Psychology with a Master's degree in Community Counseling. While in grad school, and working at a cosmetics retail store, I met a manager of a high end shoe store. Julie Wade was so impressed with my customer service skills that she offered me a job on the spot. I accepted the offer, and she allowed me to create my own schedule. At that point I realized that I could do many things and still create the life I wanted to live. I was working in a shoe store and was always interested in what it would be like to walk in someone else's shoes; a lawyer's shoes...a nurse's shoes...etc. In the meantime, I also attended many charity and networking events and it was after that when I developed "In Her Shoes Foundation," which focuses on women's empowerment, leadership and philanthropy.

I have provided clinical mental health counseling and crisis intervention to a culturally diverse population serving the South Side of Chicago and the North Shore area. I also have a history of working in various settings including the mental health court system with Cook County jail, hospital emergency rooms, community mental health agencies, and both inpatient and outpatient psychiatric hospital settings. I have served on multiple committees, the NAMI-Metro Sub Board, volunteered with the Sheliah Doyle Foundation, and was President of the Chicago Counseling Association. In 2014, Ling-Yi Zhou, my mentor and former professor invited me to teach and

I became a professor at the University of St. Francis, teaching what I'm most passionate about. The class was entitled Introduction to Crisis Intervention.

Moving on, I discovered the importance of self-care. I went on a one-month Sabbatical, to take a break from all my work and I studied yoga. After completing a 200-hour yoga certification from Zen Den Yoga School in Florida, I began to realize how important the relationship is between the mind and body.

Completing the certification and finding the work-life balance to be so important, was the reason I became a yoga instructor. I continue to deepen my knowledge of yoga by attending local classes and seminars while incorporating this knowledge in my personal and professional endeavors.

Along the way I have learned a lot about leadership. First and foremost, being a leader requires discipline, commitment, and accountability.

It takes determination and striving to be the best. There is nothing easy about being a great leader, and in the end it is your responsibility to get the job done. It is important to have a daily routine, but leave room for flexibility and unexpectedness. At least once a day someone asks me to do something or to be somewhere. I still finish everything I need to finish, but by leaving some room, I can help that person out, who will--in turn--return the favor. This is key because relationships are extremely important. The saying, "It isn't what you know but who you know," definitely holds truth; however, the best leaders are those who possess both the "what" and "who." With the "who" it is important to have strong boundaries and a strong support system. I particularly like the quote by Jim Rohn, "You are the average of the five people you spend the most time with." With open minds we can give and take so much from one another, and when we are careful we take the best qualities. This also requires being receptive to feedback. The most important, which I urge everyone to follow, is to just be yourself. Every one of us is unique and has something special to offer. It is in that uniqueness where you are most creative.

What I'm best at is giving hope, which is what I do most in my practices with crisis victims, and why I founded *In Her Shoes Foundation*. Hope is the most important thing in the world. It makes people strive for better tomorrows and change situations. It allows people to still see the light when they are so shackled in darkness even when they don't know which way to turn. Hope allows people to climb up and make something with their lives. To go after their dreams ... To me, if I get my crisis victims to see even that one speck of light, that little bit of hope, then I know I've done my job right because where there is hope, I know there is still a possibility for change. The best part of my days is knowing that if I can provide that speck of light to someone. Having the ability to remind them that life is beautiful and though it may be hard, there is still love, peace and happiness despite all the darkness, then that makes my work worthwhile. My organization, in a way, provides me with that same hope. I founded *In Her Shoes Foundation* as a positive support system to balance out the heavy themes (or times) I was dealing with in my everyday life.

I'm proud to say our organization has done nothing less--these women lift me and support me (and others) every day. They are my anchor and my inspiration. They keep me going and on course toward my dreams to make this world a better place than when I first entered into it, for which I'm extremely grateful. I encourage everyone to remain driven and dedicated to the profession. This drive and dedication manifest themselves in a delightful manner that is key in working with a wide variety of personalities and situations. In January 2015, my entrepreneurial spirit continued as I co-founded *Counseling Speaks*.

Love all and happiness is about being genuine and kind to others, being your natural self, loving what you do and sharing it with others....

Cover photo credit: Barbara Gasior Photography

13

The Power (and Profit) in Partnership
Summer Alexander and
Laura E. Knights, LCSW
"The Savvy Solopreneurs"

• • •

Long nights. Juggling one million tasks. Endless ideas and strategies to implement. Operating as the CEO and the janitor. You may know this story. This is the story of the solopreneur in the start-up phase of their business. If you are one of the fortunate ones, you will eventually come up with systems and strategies to streamline your process before you burn out. You may even hire someone down the line, but right now, in the thick of this story, it's tough. It's hard to build a sustainable and profitable business by yourself.

We both know this story all too well. Through implementing internal systems, hiring our own business coaches, outsourcing non-critical tasks, and pulling on help from virtual assistants; we were able to grow our businesses as solopreneurs without losing our sanity. However, it was (and still is) an uphill climb. Summer was managing her marketing consultancy, and Laura was managing her small business coaching and consulting practice. And then, our paths crossed.

An unexpected blessing
In 2013, while attending a small business expo in Chicago, we both listened in as the keynote speaker, Roland Martin of CNN and TV One fame, emphasized the importance of micro business owners partnering together in order to boost their economic presence faster and more effectively.

Little did we know that a year later, what was supposed to be a one-time collaboration on a virtual business training, would actually give birth to an ongoing partnership under the banner of Savvy Solopreneur Success. Together we have developed training programs, events, and other services that help solo-business owners get the systems, strategy, and support they need to move their businesses forward without losing their sanity in the process.

Keeping our individual businesses intact, we made a decision to work together on all offerings where our target audience overlapped. We believe that there is power and profit in partnership and our goal is to empower small businesses to unite instead of compete, while having a little bit of fun in the process.

Snapshot of the Solopreneur
We love helping solopreneurs because as solopreneurs ourselves we understand the challenges they face. Let's clarify what we mean by solopreneur. A

solopreneur is an individual owner of a business who is the sole employee. According to the 2014 MBO Partners State of Independence report, as of 2014 there are 30 million solo-business workers in the United States. Of those, 17.9 million regularly work 15 or more hours per week on their business while the remaining "side-giggers" work an average of 11 hours each week. This number is expected to grow with an estimated forecast of 24.5 million 15+ hour independent workers by 2019.

Although many people have taken the leap of faith to start their own businesses, the solopreneur faces many unique challenges. When you have to be the CEO, the employee, and the janitor; there are many competing responsibilities to navigate.

And often this "multiple personality" situation is unavoidable. We all know that much of those early start up years are experienced in the red, and don't leave much funds for the solopreneur to hire staff. Those that push past burnout and premature business closure, often find that their work schedule for their business is so unmanageable that essentially they just bought themselves another job.

The rate of burnout for solopreneurs is high, as the prize of achieving time, freedom, financial abundance, and/or quitting a nine-to-five job, appears to be on the other side of working nonstop hours to get your business off the ground. We often talk about burnout in flippant terms, but burnout is real.

Burnout is a state of emotional, mental, and physical exhaustion caused by excessive and prolonged stress. When you are in a state of burnout, you often feel overwhelmed and unable to meet constant demands. Many solopreneurs who experience burnout begin to lose interest and the motivation that led them to start their business in the first place. It's definitely not a positive result and you want to avoid burnout at all costs.

We've found that partnering together has helped us fight back against burnout, and boost productivity and profitability.

The Case for Partnership
Given this, we highly encourage solopreneurs to look for opportunities with other solopreneurs to ease the weight of these challenges. We've personally experienced the benefits of partnership from our collaboration.

Specifically, we've experience three major benefits of partnering together in our company, *Savvy Solopreneur Success*--pooling resources, synergy, and increased productivity.

Pooling Resources
One of the major challenges for solopreneurs in the start-up phase is having access to adequate capital to get their business off the ground. Depending on what type of business you have, you may need to stock up on inventory, invest in technological resources, purchase office space, hire consultants with special expertise, etc. Without outside investors or your own nest egg, and can

be difficult to set your business up for success if you don't have the appropriate financial footing.

For example, let's consider the customized jewelry maker. In this (and any other) supply-heavy business model, she will make the most profit from buying her jewels, chains, and other supplies in bulk. Purchasing these supplies in small quantities, let's say for just a few orders at a time, will leave her a very small margin to pull her profit from. She may literally only make pennies on the dollar without the purchasing power to get wholesale prices on her supplies. Now, combining forces and purchasing power, with another solopreneur in the industry, may allow both of them to make more profit together than they would have made separately.

Unless you are in a business that doesn't require a lot of money to get started, pooling your resources and sharing these expenses with a partner, can help you to move forward faster without draining all of your resources. For Savvy Solopreneur Success, we have pooled our resources to purchase website and graphic design resources, invest in professional development, hire a virtual assistant, get marketing materials, secure event and meeting space, and more. We've been able to stretch our dollars and keep more money in our pockets.

Synergy
Two minds are better than one. Synergy, or the increased effectiveness that results when two or more people or businesses work together, is a major benefit of partnership.

The diversity of ideas, strategies, and perspectives that emerge from different people with different experiences and expertise can skyrocket the effectiveness and profitability of your business. We have complimenting strengths. Summer is a research whiz, Laura is a visionary, and we are both quick to move to implementation. Together, these strengths are explosive. We can go from brainstorming an idea, researching it, identifying tools to implement it, and selling it to our ideal client in a matter of a day! That process may have taken two or three times as long to implement if we were working independently on the same idea.

Increased Productivity
For every entrepreneur, accountability is critical for success. It's easier to get lazy, overwhelmed, or just lost in your to-do list when working by yourself. When you have a partner and someone to be accountable to for specific tasks that were assigned to you, there's more pressure to hit the deadline when someone else's bottom line is dependent on you. Much of it is ego. Read: *"I'm not going to be the slacker of the group."* Whatever the case, we've found that working together lights a fire under our butts to get our portion of the work done when we hold each other accountable.

What's Your Partnership Style?
When solopreneurs decide to partner they put themselves in a position to expand their clientele, increase their income and provide added value to their clients all while sharing the often overwhelming workload. Yet often times solopreneurs shy away from potential partnering for fear of losing their identity.

Partnering does not have to be a permanent solution; in fact, there are a number of ways for solopreneurs to help each other. Three of the most common types of partnership are Joint Ventures, Strategic Partnerships, and Subcontracting.

With joint venture partnerships, each party decides to work together for a defined period of time. You may decide to host a live event, run a virtual training program or bid on a larger corporate contract together. Joint ventures are great for partnering with another solopreneur who offers a specific and unique set of skills and expertise that you do not currently possess.

A strategic partnership is an alliance between two businesses typically over a prolonged period of time. Typically with this kind of partnership each partner is currently serving the same ideal clients in different but complementary ways. For example if you own a catering company perhaps you would form a strategic partnership with an event planner. This allows you to have and give trusted referrals.

If you would like to try partnering but do not want to commit to a joint venture or strategic partnership, a subcontractor arrangement might be ideal for you. With this kind of partnership another business owner will do the work necessary to secure clients and hire you to fulfill a smaller portion the contract. This is great for solopreneurs who struggle with the sales and marketing functions of their businesses but are great at what they do.

Getting Ready for Partner

We encourage all of our solopreneur clients to look for ways to partner with other solopreneurs for all the reasons we've mentioned above. If you think you may be ready to take on a partner, here are a few points to help you do some self-assessment:

You are clear on your business model. You know who your ideal clients are, can clearly state your offerings and the benefits and features of each one, and have a clear picture of your finances including revenue, expenses, and profit.

You can directly connect partnering with increasing your profitability. Partnering is not just about making new friends (although we hope you do!). Partnering is ultimately about helping you make more money more effectively and efficiently than you would have done on your own. If you cannot make a concrete link between partnering and increasing revenue in your business, it does not make sense to enter into a partnership.

You can share the spotlight with another talented entrepreneur. Depending on what type of partnership you engage in, you may have to share the spotlight. In our business, we share the stage and it requires a certain level of confidence and security that allows us to not be threatened by the other's success. You will need to check your ego at the door in order for a partnership to be successful.

You can clearly state the expectations for what you want to get out of the partnership. Clarifying your expectations and being able to verbally state them to your partner is a foundation for success in any relationship, including a business partnership. Clear expectations will allow you and your partner to be on the same page when creating goals for the partnership and identifying the roles of responsibilities of each person.

If you find that you could not confidently answer "YES" to all of these statements, we recommend that you re-examine your thoughts about your business goals before pursuing partnership opportunities. It will be critical for you to have clarity in these areas for your business and your partnership efforts to be enjoyable for you and profitable for your business.

Finding a Partner
If you passed the self-assessment test and feel that you are ready to move forward, here are a few recommended steps for finding a partner:

Review the different types of partnerships we discussed above, and identify which one may fit your business at this time.

Brainstorm a list of partner qualities that are attractive to you. This could include type of business, specific industry, type of client served, revenue range, work style, market reputation, skill sets or areas of expertise, location, etc. Be sure to consider qualities that are "on your level." You want the partnership to be mutually beneficial and not draining to any one person. Each partner should bring something of equivalent value to the other, and both parties should be able to learn from the other.

Now that you have a list of qualities for an ideal partner, brainstorm a list of people that may meet some of the characteristics. Of course, you will have to do some more investigation here, but just create a draft list of people/businesses to explore.

Once you've identified a few people, send an email sharing your thoughts with an invitation to talk more. Or, jump on the phone for a brief conversation, and then try to schedule a follow up meeting to discuss more in detail. Once there's some mutual interest in partnering, meeting up at a restaurant, coffee house, or Skype to discuss a potential partnership is a great first "business date."

At the meeting, have some dialogue together and brainstorm the possibilities for a potential partnership. Run your partner through the same assessment points you reflected on above. Explore the numbers together, as well as potential projects. It's also important to listen to yourself. What energy are you picking up from the other person? Does the flow of the conversation feel good to you? What's your gut response to the ideas shared about a potential partnership?

If there's mutual interest with moving forward, document your partnership with a legal agreement that details profit share agreements, roles and responsibilities, and the time frame for the agreement. We provide more information on this below.

Set your timeline, revenue goals, client targets, etc. and get to work!

Managing the Partnership

Once you've found the perfect partner for your solo business it will be important to manage the partnership effectively. In what we lovingly refer to as the "Rock Band Theory," we've found that it can be difficult to keep a partnership intact for a number of reasons. When you think about some of the most famous bands in history such as The Police, you saw the destruction of a partnership filled with talented people because of personality clashes and egos.

In order to form a successful partnership whether for a one-time collaboration or an ongoing effort you need to have a few key components in place. While you don't have to be clones of each other it will be important that you have some shared values and viewpoints as it relates to business. You'll also want to have an established level of trust, as there will be money involved.

A Few More Considerations...

So, we have provided a pretty compelling argument for why you should consider partnering with another solo-business owner; however, before we end our chapter, we have a few more important considerations to share with you.

Here is your official disclaimer: We are not qualified to give you any legal or financial advice for your business, and these points are not intended to do so. Always consult your legal, tax, and financial advisors before making any major decisions for your business.

Ok, not that we've got that out of the way, we would be remiss if we didn't strongly encourage you to have an official legal contract in place for your agreement. Be sure to cover all the bases to protect yourself upfront and to be completely transparent from the onset of your partnership. Our agreement covers areas like ownership percentages for our joint initiative; how liabilities, expenses, and work responsibilities will be handled; profit share specifications; branding; terms and cancellation restrictions, dispute resolution terms, and more. Did we go into the partnership, expecting to have to take each other to court? Absolutely not. But as smart businesswomen, we understand that it's better to be safe than sorry, especially when our assets, brands, and business reputations are on the line. We encourage you to do the same. Your lawyer can assist you with creating an agreement or you can use one of the more affordable lawyer-reviewed, done-for-you services that exist.

Like any type of relationship, compatibility is important but nothing is perfect without putting forth effort. In business and in life, integrity will take you a long way. Don't be so quick to give up if you can see the benefit on your bottom line. If after multiple attempts to make it work, you find it more stressful for you to keep the partnership than to let it go; don't be afraid to cut your losses and dissolve the partnership... just be sure to be professional in your approach and to cover stipulations for ending the partnership in your legal agreement.

And remember, just because it didn't work with one person doesn't mean it can't work with another. Keep your eyes and ears open for other potential partners that may be a better fit for you.

Happy Partnering and Business Blessings!

14

Starting and Running My Businesses
Daniel C. Lewis

"Opportunity is missed by most people because it is dressed in overalls and looks like work." - *Thomas Edison*

• • •

At some point everyone on some level has the desire to start and manage their own business. As you're reading this now, I am sure some of those strong desires to start and own your own business are resurfacing. My desires to start my own business became stronger and stronger as each year passed. Once I started the process and transformation from working for a corporation in a middle management position to becoming self-employed with my own company to becoming a business owner with several businesses, my life took off. Being a business owner really gave me a sense of pride in myself and my abilities.

If you are considering starting and running your own business you have to start with the basic question. This basic question has been asked by every successful business owner in the world in one form or another. This basic question will determine how you get up in the morning and how and when you go to bed at night. This basic question should be asked before you do anything relative to the start of the business and that includes writing a business plan. This question will determine the success or the failure of your business.

The basic question is:

"Why do you want to start a business?"

Take the next 60 seconds and write down your "Why?"

_____

_____

_____

Your "Why" is so critically important to your success. Your "Why" will determine your energy level in the morning as well as at night before you go to bed. Your "Why" will determine what you will focus on as you write your business plan. Your "Why?" will determine if you will still be in business five years from now. Your "Why?" will determine what goals you are willing to actually set and attain in this business endeavor.

Some successful business people have said paying your dues or going through a certain amount of struggling is on the road to your successfully achieving your goals. Others would say it is more of making the appropriate sacrifices to achieve your goals. Despite how you would phrase it, there is time and effort that goes into all success.

"To make profound changes in your life, you need either inspiration or desperation." By Anthony Robbins

I have been very fortunate to have traveled across the country conducting workshops on how to building a business. This has given me the privilege of meeting several new business professionals. These business professionals came from a variety of different communities both rural as well as urban. Small towns like Orangeburg, South Carolina and Seaside, Oregon to big cities like New York, New York, San Francisco, California, and Indianapolis, Indiana. While talking with these business professionals I have found that they have all entered self-employment a variety of ways.

Developing a business can be a daunting task. What type of business should you have? Sole Proprietorships? LLC? S Corporation? What about financing your venture or compensating yourself? What about obtaining the proper licensing, permits and preparing for taxes? One thing that is for sure.....there is no consistent way to start a notary business.

Here are four suggested steps that potential new business owners can take in order to improve their success as a business owner. These steps are designed to increase success while lowering failure rates for your business. The following four suggested methods to starting a successful business are:

1. **Write a business plan**. Writing a business plan forces you to review every aspect of your business. A business plan will help you gain clarity about your business, gain a deeper understanding about your market, stay organized, allows you to question the validity of your actions, as well as establish certain key benchmarks for your business. Many people including myself when starting out didn't know quite how to write a business plan. This is why I recommend using SCORE.

Score is a nonprofit association dedicated to helping small businesses get off the ground, grow and achieve their goals through education and mentorship. SCORE is considered the most trusted source for small business plans. SCORE offers free webinars, business advisors who can help you formulate a great business plan. Check their website for more details at www.score.org.

2. **Find a mentor**. Mentoring starts with getting paired with an experienced, successful business owner. Mentoring can substantially increase your chances to build a successful business. Mentoring facilitates sharing knowledge, expertise, skills, insights, and experiences through dialogue and collaborative learning.

Mentoring also encourages engagement, developing an effective day-to-day business strategy and encourages continual learning. I would encourage everyone to join a local or national professional association to find a proper mentor. The best and brightest business professionals usually belong to a professional business association. Attending local and national association workshops gives you a great pool of prospects.

3. **Plug-in to self-development**. Self-development is about investing in yourself so that you can effectively manage yourself regardless of the situation. Self-development means taking the time and making the commitment, to invest in your greatest resource – you. Personal business effectiveness is proportionate to the level of committed self-development. Self-development could mean something as tangible as a few sacrifices made in order to have your business run efficiently as well as effectively. For example, in order to become better at social media marketing you may want to get up earlier each day and read a marketing book for 5 – 10 minutes on how to do so. A couple of great books on social media marketing by the way are "Get Rich Click" by Marc Ostrofsky and "Guerilla Marketing" by Jay Conrad Levinson.

Self-development has been compared many times to going to an auction. It is an exciting time at the beginning of the auction like it is when you start your business. When the bidding opens everyone is bidding because the bidding starts low so everyone can take part. As the price gets higher and higher what usually happens? Fewer and fewer people will bid. Compared to having a new business as compliance guides come into place and it becomes tougher and tougher to comply with regulations fewer and fewer notaries are available for assignments. Self-development will help keep you at that business professional level that the new business requires.

153

4. **Join a national or local notary association.** Joining a national or local professional association can also assist with finding an acceptable mentor. Not only that, an association can assist with keeping you up to date on new laws as well as compliance issues, assist with professional development workshops, and networking opportunities. Several associations will even give to the local community by sponsoring scholarships and grants. Belonging to an association in addition to the other benefits protects and promotes your profession.

Remember all of us have our own personality and our own life experiences. Doing these four things doesn't guarantee you success, but it does lower your notary business at chances of being unsuccessful.

Daniel C. Lewis is a nationally recognized speaker. He has conducted workshops all over the country. He has mentored many new and upcoming business owners.

An entrepreneur, business executive, instructional filmmaker, social media expert and strategic consultant Daniel addresses innovation within a diverse range of topics.

Daniel received national acclaim by being selected as the 2010 Notary of the Year by the National Notary Association. In the same year he was honored by the Indiana Secretary of State as an Honorary Secretary of State.

15

To Begin ~ You Must Begin
Marti Hannon

• • •

When Julie asked me to write my story in TEW 3; I balked and said, "I'm not an entrepreneur yet, I haven't even begun." She responded, "That is your chapter, To begin, you must begin." Well, what does that mean?

To begin one must have a dream and a vision. Up until recently, I didn't have a vision. I had stopped dreaming. I was caught in the endless trudge of stress and self-inflicted work martyrdom. There was no time and energy to dream. I strived to just survive each day. It felt like an existence rather than living. My life was a perpetual circular door of taking care of others. I had started pursuing a career of serving others at an early age. I helped to take care my mom and then she died of cancer by the time I was seventeen. I had planned on being a nurse, in the mission field, long before she was sick. I had just decided that was how I would serve the Lord. After she passed away, my life took many twists and turns.

As soon as I graduated high school I supported myself and worked 2-3 jobs at a time. I kept pushing to complete prerequisite courses for nursing. I worked as a nurses aide in every aspect of healthcare and home care. I filled in some hours as an activity aide along with many other jobs. After a serious neck, back, and knee injuries I had to re-evaluate my career choice. It was during this time that I finally asked the Lord what He wanted me to do with my life. One day the answer came clearly through my dad. He said to me, "Have you thought about being an activity director or a kindergarten teacher?" I hadn't thought of that, but the minute he said activity director, my entire life came into focus. I quickly finished a Bachelor's of Science degree in Therapeutic Recreation. All of those nursing pre-requisites were needed for that degree as well. As a Recreational Therapist, I was really good at helping individuals overcome the obstacles and barriers in their way of living to their potential.

I became immersed in my profession, working in different aspects of recreational therapy and ultimately activity consulting in older adult residential communities. I loved that my work helped restore: hope, purpose, dreams, love, and life to people. Ironically, there wasn't room in my heart and mind to dream. I was not walking my talk. Somewhere along my journey, I lost myself in the care of others. There was a nagging ache in my heart that something was wrong and I wanted more. For several years, I kept thinking, "I want a different life". I had lost faith that plans made would come to fruition.

I was afraid to make goals because I thought I would fail. In my mind it was better to not set myself up for failure. My work and profession was safe and secure. Therefore, I didn't allow myself to dream.

To dream or not to dream really comes down to the question, Am I willing to fail? What happens if I fail? I'm embarrassed, a disappointment, jobless, not able to pay bills, lose credibility, lose acceptance, experience pain and rejection, and need to start over. I had this unfounded belief that I had to make it on my own strength, of which I had no confidence. I was afraid.

Fear is the biggest obstacle of beginning. This quote from the movie After Earth provided me with an important perspective on fear, Cypher Raige said to his son, "Fear is not real. The only place that fear can exist is in our thoughts of the future. It is a product of our imagination, causing us to fear things that do not at present and may not ever exist. That is near insanity Kitai. Do not misunderstand me, danger is very real, but fear is a choice. We are telling ourselves a story and that day mine changed." Quote retrieved from http://www.imdb.com/title/tt1815862/quotes.

What was the story I had been telling myself? That I would fail and it would be better to not try, then to try and fail. I was afraid of uncertainty and the insecurity that comes with stepping into a new adventure. Before I could be free of the fear that plagued me; I had to identify where the fear originated.

Indulge me as I review my adult existence. I lost my mom to cancer when I was 17. Within 4 months my dad met his future wife. He was engaged a month later and was married a few months after that. Before the one year anniversary of my mom's death: my father remarried, I had to move in with my stepmother, my life was disassembled, memories sold in a garage sale, and my dog put to sleep, I then moved again into my best friend's home. I worked hard in the local hospital and somehow I completed high school. From 1993 to 2003; I had a friend die in my arms, I moved 11 times, held 11 different jobs (2-3 at a time), and attended 5 colleges. From 2003-2013 I moved again, graduated with honors from college, and held another 10 jobs. In 2012 I started to have panic attacks and apathy toward work that I typically loved. I've come to realize that acceptance, belonging, stability, and security are all very important to me as they are to most people. All the change and instability caught up with me. These needs not being met was keeping me from stepping into the world of possibility.

Freedom to dream, walk in faith, and live to my full potential was a distant dream of a dream. While I lived under the bondage of my past, I couldn't even glimpse in the direction of that dream. I was stuck and I didn't know how to move forward. I wanted a different life, a fresh start, a brand new perspective, and nothing happened. While longing to be free, I clung to my faith and the Lord held me tight. On January 1st, 2013, a little after midnight, my perspective began to change after writing a poem that reflected the true state of my heart and mind. I was ashamed of the way I was living, I knew fear was keeping me from living in the full freedom that comes from belonging to the Lord. I couldn't understand why, and felt tremendous guilt that a woman of faith could be bound by fear. The Lord spoke to me in that painful place.

I felt these words in my heart, "You are mine, I called you by name and knew you before you had form. I am pleased with my creation. I am glorified in you, because I created you. Therefore your very existence cries out in joy. You cannot stop me from being glorified in you. It happens automatically. You are covered in my spirit and truth. My angels guard over you. My precious one, my beautiful one…rise up and be discouraged no more. I, who formed you have done a good work in you. You are who I intended you to be. Be free in that. Be free and know I am God. I will accomplish what I have set forth to do through you. Be not afraid or ashamed. You are safe in me. Nothing you do can bring me shame. You cannot stop me from doing what I have planned for you. You will not. I will…because I AM. Rest in that and know that I AM."

Thus began my journey of awareness and healing. The Lord brought an amazing therapist to walk the journey with me. Dr. Bernada Nicole Baker helped me to face the loss, pain, and grief which had been masked by: seeking acceptance in my accomplishments, making work my life, constant change, and care giving. For a year, she had been encouraging me to assemble a vision board. I was afraid to even do that. Just before the New Year in 2015, I went away on a weekend getaway. My goal was to review the work and healing that had taken place over the past year and complete that vision board. It was remarkable to realize how far I had come in my journey toward freedom. The last night, I finally took out the supplies and materials to work on the board. This simple act caused so much fear to rise up. The stories of fear that I was telling myself included, "What if I put it on the board and it doesn't happen?" and "I won't be able to do that, I have tried before and failed." I quieted those wrong thoughts and just went about the task in front of me. Once I started, excitement took hold and I stayed up all night until I finished my dreaming. Completing that vision board threw open the doors in my mind to a life of endless possibilities.

Now I see opportunities everywhere. I am no longer feeling stuck but am beginning to live freely in a new adventure. This victory was not easily won and I have to continually fight to remain living free. The change of mindset and perspective is just the beginning. To truly live in the realm of possibility that pushes an entrepreneur to do; you have to remain intentional in living an authentic and balanced life. If you are stuck at a life obstacle: you have to evaluate why, get support, implement a solution, do the work, and move forward. If you fall, do what I do and hit the life "ctrl-alt-dlt" buttons.

I easily lose focus and go back to my old familiar routine. Taking on too many projects that are not meaningful to me, exhausting myself by meeting other's needs, and then going brain dead when I get home. That is not living and I don't ever want to go back. I have to be purposeful investing in my well-being and future. I want to and I will move beyond the beginning. It's time to launch into the stratosphere of my dreams.

After writing the first draft of this chapter I took a very brave step, I registered my business name with the government. World Changer Consulting will work to empower providers of aging services to interact with individuals in meaningful and engaging methods. My entire life has led to this point of living in my purpose. I have put in my notice to a great job that has sheltered and taught me so much. After five years of belonging to an amazing team, I am stepping out into a new world and way of living.

The minute I put in my notice, doors opened and I truly have been launched in the stratosphere. Three national companies are committed to working with me in empowering, educating, equipping, and encouraging care providers. I am being handed the opportunity to truly create change for older adults and the way the world interacts with them. I got out of my own way and the Lord was able to release the plans He had in store for me. My Lord, a great therapist, and intentional life work have brought me to a better place.

What about you? Have you stopped dreaming? What has led you to this point? What is holding you back? What can you do differently today to start living your dream?

Let me conclude with the following thoughts from Maya Angelou:

"You may not control all the events that happen to you.

But you can decide not to be reduced by them."

"You may encounter many defeats but you must not be defeated."

"Hope and fear cannot occupy the same space at the same time. Invite one to stay."

"My mission in life is not merely to survive, but to thrive, and to do so with some passion, some compassion, some humor, and some style."

May the joy of the Lord shine upon you and make your path straight in the name of Jesus!

Go change the World!
Marti Hannon C.T.R.S.
Founder of World Changer Consulting
www.worldchangerconsulting.com

16

THE TRUTH ABOUT ENTREPRENEURSHIP©
Angelia Hopson

"In this life, I have worn many hats from corporate employee to entrepreneur and feel that all of those experiences have led me to this work of passion!"

● ● ●

Angelia has worked for many years with, for and on behalf of small and minority businesses, serving on various committees and boards that support small business. For over 15 years she has worked with CMSDC (Chicago Minority Supplier Development Council); HMSDC (Houston Minority Supplier Development Council); Chicago MBDA (Minority Business Development Agency) and WIPP (Women Impacting Public Policy). She has been an entrepreneur for over 18 years. She has received several awards, most notably Contractor of the Year by MBDA.

She is a virulent advocate for small business taking on organizations and individuals that threaten the existence and viability of small business. Every institution needs its champion and Angelia has a winning record taking a stand and raising awareness about disparities impacting small and minority business. The challenge has had peaks and valleys, but the rewards have cultivated a dedication to the cause to which she volunteers tirelessly.

Angelia is currently the Chief Strategist for iCoach360, a boutique firm that specializes in bringing entrepreneurs together for education, business development, leadership training, and networking, which functions as a reference for small businesses to gain insight on a multitude of issues affecting entrepreneurial businesses. The education, whether formal training or mastermind sessions, have real life, tangible impact on the businesses and people who participate.

A simple dedication to the cause is not enough to make a good business coach or entrepreneurial leader. You have to have experienced the trials and tribulations of business ownership. Angelia has owned, developed, and bought and sold businesses for years, which have resulted in **seven figure** contracts with clients including Wal-Mart/Sam's Club, UPS, City of Chicago, ComEd, Albertson's, BP (Deep Water Horizon Oil Spill), Super Storm Sandy Recovery teams and many more. This type of expertise cannot be purchased, it has to be lived. Her extensive breadth and depth of knowledge is far ranging whether to guide business owners strategically or navigationally, or both. A benefit of working with Angelia is the startling array of contacts she has and can possibly connect you with.

Her ability to communicate to individuals and large groups and to connect on a personal level has been demonstrated through many public speaking engagements. She has lectured, taught and spoken to groups for College of DuPage, the CMSDC, the US Postal Service, the City of Milwaukee, women's business groups and several large religious groups on topics including entrepreneurship, leadership, sales and business development, marketing and branding, occupational safety as well as application of spiritual teachings to create your best life.

Ms. Hopson is a second generation entrepreneur. Her parents owned and operated a print press and Christian Bookstore, whose philosophy of business fully embraced a quote by Dr. John C. Maxwell: ***"The Dream is free, but the journey isn't."*** Angelia firmly believes life is about doing, not waiting or wanting but actually doing and creating the life you dream about. She is a graduate of both Robert Morris College and the Tuck School of Business Executive Training.

"At iCoach360, we take entrepreneurs from dreaming to doing!"

When most new entrepreneurs talk about entrepreneurship they usually talk about it in all its glory...the passion, the freedom, removing the proverbial income cap, they walk around spouting phrases like, "When you do what you love, you'll never work another day in your life", "Success leave clues", or "What's your why?" However, I think the best phrase I've heard lately that sums up entrepreneurship for me was made by my brother, "The Believe Coach", Nicholas Dillon – "You can't be new to it, you gotta be true to it."

Well, I'm certainly not new to it and I'm definitely true to it.

FIRST TRUTH ABOUT ENTREPRENEURSHIP IS, IT'S ALL HARD!

Let's take a step back. After your chance to read my bio on the previous page, let me give you some background not encompassed in a professional bio – let me tell you more about who I am and where I'm from. Born in rural Mississippi in the 1960s, right in the middle of the Civil Rights Movement, to Christian parents who were also entrepreneurs. By the time I came along, they had already fought the good fight of entrepreneurship and we were able to enjoy the fruits of their labor. My dad was buying homes and cars for cash, had money in every bank in our small town. He was a pastor of the local church and we owned a Christian bookstore and print press where he printed everything from Sunday School Books to usher badges.

I'm convinced entrepreneurs are born and not made; it is an unquenchable fire in your belly, burning with purpose and passion. I've had quite a few jobs in my career and though I have excelled at each of them, gained notoriety, reached higher levels that my colleagues, captured promotions and bonuses, I've never been truly happy as an employee.

The theory of "never working another day in your life" is a farce...you will never work harder at anything more than building a business. It consists of long days and longer nights, planning, creating, strategizing. It includes working in all the aspects of your business...unless you launch with an incredible amount of capital reserves, you will be administrative assistant, marketing guru, master networker, salesperson and account executive as well as book keeper and compliance officer all the while balancing both human and financial resources.

When I started my first business in 1998 I wish someone would have told me just how many balls I needed to juggle alone to make a real go of it. It's time entrepreneurs, real entrepreneurs, tell the truth about just how difficult it is to launch and grow a business. I don't tell this story to depress or discourage you from starting a business, but simply to help clear the smoke so you go into it eyes wide open. The passion to help entrepreneurs go from dreaming to doing with realistic expectations is the foundation of iCoach30. I firmly believe by being honest about the challenges and helping entrepreneurs navigate the complexity we can stop the chaos and slow the rate of small business failure.

Let's take a look at the numbers:

Every year 400,000 small businesses open and 470,000 close.

The United States is 12th in the world for producing entrepreneurs.

In America, there are 26 million businesses at any given time and though this sounds like an impressive number, let's look closer –

- Of the 26 million businesses in America, there are only 6 million that have one or more employees.

- Of those 6 million, only 3.8 million have four or fewer employees.

- There are about a million companies with five to nine employees.

- There are 600,000 companies with 10 – 19 employees.

- There are also 500,000 companies with 20 – 99 employees.

- There are 90,000 businesses with 100 to 499 employees.

- Only 18,000 with 500 or more employees.

You can see by the numbers there is a distinct difference between the people building businesses and the people building lifestyles. Lifestyle entrepreneurs typically don't have employees, they are the people who plug into big network marketing groups that convince them they are entrepreneurs...and though there is a lot of money to be made in those plug-in businesses, it is not one of true entrepreneurial grit.

Next, there is also a big difference between an entrepreneur who starts a business and one who buys a business such as succeeding a parent who founded a company or buying the business they used to work for or buying into a franchise (another topic for later.)

These are the real odds of entrepreneurial success, and it is clear that somebody needs to tell the truth about entrepreneurship...and I'm that somebody. With nearly 20 years of entrepreneurial experience and having employed up to 75 employees at one time, I have defied many of the odds.

This journey is much harder than anyone lets on, but there is as much reward as there is risk, so let's unpack it.

Let's Unpack 5 Truths About Entrepreneurship

Truth #1 - Money May Not Be On The List

When I began my first business, I was so excited; I had a metal desk and a telephone set   up initially in a spare bedroom, then in an unfinished basement. It's 1998 and I was sitting there with my new computer, all 264k of memory and a two line phone with the misconception that somehow since I was excited, had exerted so much energy planning and dreaming that miraculously clients would know I was in business, but the phone wasn't ringing.

So I began to look at my plans again, figure out a marketing strategy and make a list of everything I hoped to garner from being an entrepreneur. My list included things like autonomy of my time, control of my income, freedom to build something from nothing and it went on. The most important thing on the list was autonomy as I was raising my son and I wanted to be available to him and for him...for field trips and school plays. Later I would come to realize it was not about the field trips and school plays but that deep desire for autonomy was God's way of preparing me for the journey ahead (we'll talk about that a little more later).

Years later, I pulled out that initial list and realized I never put money on the list as a priority for owning my business. Though I made millions over the years, the priority was my family. Today's list is very different and your list should evolve as you do and as your business does. Every entrepreneur has their "why" for starting a business. You should know it from the onset but realize it will change as the years go on. My son is grown now, therefore the need for autonomy is less and the need for legacy and financial stability is greater. Keep the list handy and review it often, it is what drives you toward your goals.

Takeaway: Make a list that reflects your deepest desires for your life first. Your business goals should line up with and support your life goals. If you are only in it for the money, you are in it for the wrong reason. Financial gain only is for investors not entrepreneurs. Which are you?

Truth #2 - You Must Be A Self-Starter

During the basement years, I was very disciplined. My friends and family fondly refer to me as "The Colonel" if that's any indication. I started my day the same as when I worked for a large corporation - I prepared for the day the evening before, laying out my clothes and writing down my list of to-do's. When my feet hit the floor I followed my normal morning ritual, got dressed and applied full makeup just to walk to the other side of the house and down to the unfinished basement that was my office. I only allowed myself to walk back upstairs for two reasons – the bathroom or the garage to leave for a client meeting. I contend this kind of discipline is necessary to succeed in a new business and especially in a home-based business that can easily be derailed by the expectations of friends and family as well as that basket of laundry that keeps luring you when you should be working.

When I left corporate America to pursue my dreams, there were five other friends that took the plunge the same year. At the time, my business was growing much faster than theirs, so they would call me for advice, "How do I get certified?", "How do I set my pricing?" or "How do I negotiate a contract with a large corporation?" I offered to help them with any knowledge I had as long as it was after 6 pm on a weekday or any time on the weekend. I could not run the risk of spending my revenue generating hours helping them grow their businesses, when I was growing my own.

Not one of them took me up on my offer of after-hours help, but when we would get together for a girl's day they would compare notes, who slept in the longest and who watched the latest Oprah show while going on and on about how I was too serious about business. Those conversations and jokes, though funny, mark a period in time for me that makes me very proud of my stick-to-it-ness. All five of those friends returned to corporate jobs and I haven't worked for anyone other than myself for nearly 20 years.

Takeaway: Don't ever let anyone rain on your parade. It all seems impossible until it's done and if you are not clear about your goals and go in hot pursuit of them, someone else will hire you to help them achieve their dreams. Dream builder or employee – your choice.

Truth #3 - People Will Think You Are Crazy!

Has anyone asked, "Why are you leaving your good job?" or made statements like, "Why are you starting a business in a down economy"? If so, welcome to entrepreneurship!

Always remember your vision and passion for the business you are embarking on is YOUR vision and passion and almost no one else will get it. Often times it's the people closest to you that struggle with your evolution from working stiff to entrepreneur. This is their issue not yours, so don't internalize how someone else feels. It's difficult for people to see you in a different light. Think about actors and actresses who are being cast in a role of a lifetime and can't seem to get other work because the audience can't see them any other way. When John Travolta was casted in Welcome Back Kotter, Saturday Night Fever and Grease in the 1970s, those roles became his persona and it took until the late 1990s before he was casted in roles like Michael, Pulp Fiction and The General's Daughter. What role have you cast yourself in? What will you need to do to change your image for entrepreneurial success?

When I first launched my business, I put a few rituals in place, some of which we talked about earlier. I followed them to the letter, no matter who called or attempted to distract me, I was laser focused on my success.

I was determined not to let the distractions of life keep me from reaching my goals. I had to devote time to training my family and friends to respect my time and how to respect my business as a REAL job! I set up the parameters around when I would take personal phone calls, when I could stop to watch TV with my family, etc. After a few months they accepted my new schedule and in nearly 20 years, I haven't had to retrain anyone. As I grew the business and stuck to my schedule, everyone else around me adapted. Remember, you teach people how to treat you.

You must know what you need to be successful and go after it with as much ferocity as you can muster. In order for me to be successful it was necessary for me to follow my daily rituals. Today, I still follow most of the rituals I put in place many years ago. When my schedule gets off track and I'm not hitting my goals, I go back to the basics and shift back into that mode of extreme focus. It's what works for me. You must identify what works for you and don't let anyone knock you off your square.

Takeaway: You are the CEO of YOU! You have the ability to design the life you desire. It will take discipline and shutting down both the voices in your head and those of the people around you, but you are capable of creating the business and life of your dreams!

173

Truth #4 - Your Personal Life Will Vanish!

When I started no one told me that my personal life would be virtually nonexistent. As a new entrepreneur you are captivated by the thrill of the game, the chase of new clients and new opportunities. It is all very exhilarating...after all you are your own boss now. Well, that quickly gets muddied by the complexity of owning a business, the paperwork to be filed with the federal, state and local government, the accountability and compliance issues that arise, you're working long hours, often traveling depending on your business, purchasing equipment, setting up systems, planning, etc. You're often distracted thinking about ways to improve, grow and survive....how to be sustainable and relevant, thinking about the problems your business has and the financial stress of it all takes a toll on your relationships.

You are the go-to person for every major decision and before you build staff that is every decision. There are times you will have to make difficult, heart wrenching, stress-inducing decisions. Decisions like, to grow or not to grow, to hire or to fire, parting ways with partners, and the list goes on. The decision to pay vendors and employees, while often times neglecting a paycheck for yourself, which presents financial strains for you personally. This must be balanced against your personal relationships...will your spouse or significant other understand the nuances of the business and the financial ebbs and flows?

Decisions, no matter how well thought out or even present, the appearance of accuracy in the moment will live to haunt you long after they have been executed and implemented. You may forever question in hindsight whether or not you made the correct decision.

Though you are enamored with the idea of entrepreneurship, the reality is every aspect of the business impacts your personal life. The long hours take time away from your family and friends. The cost of launching and sustainability impacts your personal finances. Most small businesses finance their start-up with the help of friends, family and credit cards. When you add up the time you are away and the time you are physically present but still mentally working on the business, it equates to a significant sacrifice. There are many times I had to pass on a social event to work on the business. This is often a source of contention for small business owners. Do I go to my child's school play or stay in the office to work on the business. I specifically say **ON** because, it is much more important to work **ON** your business than **IN** your business. We will talk about the difference later.

Takeaway: Remember to do what is important and not what is urgent. What seems urgent in the moment may not be important in the long run. Do not make short sighted decisions. It's much more important to plan, look at the long term effects on your business and your life and make the necessary sacrifices in the short term for the long term gain. Make a list of what is important to you and your family as you embark on this new adventure.

#5 - Nothing Happens As Quickly As You Think It Will, IF it Happens

If I had a dollar for every time I uttered the words, 'we will be starting a new project soon,' only to find out that the start date got pushed, or the project is starting but our portion's deadline isn't due until months later, or even worse, I landed the contract that was a lucrative, multi-year contract and realized the client didn't necessarily have to utilize our services until year 3, if at all! As you sit in the client's office discussing their needs or lack thereof in the moment, all the alarms are going off in your head as you maintain your cool and hope they can't read that desperate fire in your eyes.

It took me years to understand the duality of celebration after landing work. Most of my business has been done with major corporations and let me tell you now, corporations are NOT people and the people who execute these mega contracts are never emotional about the outcomes. It is very black and white, you deliver or you don't. Your contract can be fully funded and if there is a different need that is perceived to be greater than the need for your services, those resources can be reallocated overnight.

Walk with me through just one example – this multi-national, corporate giant shall remain nameless. My team and I worked on the oil spill of 2010 in the Gulf of Mexico. After the spill we began meeting with other oil and gas companies and their emergency response teams to be added to their vendor lists. When we met with executives of a certain company they proposed to hire us to develop a safety mobile app for their business. We went back to our Houston offices and started working, involving all the necessary players, attorneys, accountants, software developers and of course our safety team. We worked on the product for 18 months without before we were paid one dime, we invested $900,000 of our own money to make a go of what we knew would be an industry game changer. Finally, after adding staff, onboarding developers, writing many hours of code, working with our Chinese partner at odd hours of day and night, we received the work order that pairs our safety consulting services with our mobile app...PAYDAY!!! At the time, I had a team of 23 employees and about 10 contractors. Everyone was overjoyed; this was the day we had worked so hard for. Our contract was funded for many millions – we received our first installment for several million dollars, keep in mind, we had already invested $900,000 so the first installment is not overly exciting, but we are funded so we are good...right?!?! Wrong. We work with the client on implementation, they changed horses' mid-stream and decided to reallocate those resources. We quickly discover the second installment isn't coming. Needless to say everyone is disappointed and the business is severely impacted. What to do? Unfortunately, this happens every day to small businesses. It is the risk you take when you jump into the water with the sharks.

Takeaway: I would rather play the game and lose than to sit idly while opportunities passed me by. The learnings from this and other experiences have

prepared me to propel my business forward much faster than if I never had that experience. It was a loss and very painful, but they don't teach THIS is business school. Again, problems will always arise, and you will always have to adjust on the journey and think about how much fun you will be having as you're learning and earning.

I am grateful for the opportunity to share with you The Truth About Entrepreneurship©.

This contribution to T.E.W. (The Entrepreneur Within) is an excerpt from the upcoming book release of The Truth About Entrepreneurship©. There we will dig into some other topics such as:

- Everyone In The Boat With You Are Not Rowing

- Time Wasters and Money Thieves

- Bootstrapping 101

- Staying Power

- Networking is NOT Relationship Building

- NO is a Good Answer

- Marketing is NOT Sales

- The Dream is Free

- Let Go and Grow – The Art of Delegation…..and much, much more.

Stay tuned for the release date. In the meantime, you need to know: The road to success is not a straight line.

Success | Success

what people think | what it really
it looks like | looks like

It is jagged up, down, with lots of twists and turns. Do not get lost in the curves. Stay the course. You are well on your way and you will get there. ***"Success Is Not Permanent and Failure Is Not Fatal."*** Whatever you do, never give up. You will make mistakes, simply correct and continue.

17

Stand for Something: It's Your Business Brand!
Rai Barney, Chief HR and Business Expert – Optimal Placement Services, LLC

• • •

1: WHAT IS YOUR "WHY?"
Why do you do what you do?

Optimal Placement Services, LLC was created in 2013 and Resume' Respect Services preceded this business, established in 2006. Optimal Placement Services is a full-service career services firm specializing in recruiting, staffing, resume updates, resume creation, business/career coaching, interview preparation assistance, job search assistance and human resources consulting.

With over 10 years of progressive human resources management experience working in various industries, including consulting, banking, government, technology, manufacturing, retail, education, healthcare and non-profit, I have turned my passion into a business. I love assisting professionals and business owners with achieving their optimal level of success in their careers and businesses.

One of my biggest professional accomplishments was being the first Human Resources Manager for a 200-employee organization, where I had to create a processes and procedures manual for a human resources department. I developed their current human resources structure, wrote policies, implemented their payroll system and ensured I had buy-in from the CEO, executives and managers.

I love human resources, as people are the biggest asset for every organization. It is important that companies motivate and retain their top talent. Employees want to work for companies that value and appreciate their work and skill-set. Companies need employees to grow, in order to fulfill their mission and vision.

As an HR expert and current HR Practitioner, I work every day to advocate for employees. As a business owner, who advocates for you? No one will, so you must advocate for yourself. You must truly believe in your all skills and talents, as it is your brand. Who will believe in your brand more than you, absolutely no one!

2: WHY/HOW/WHEN DID YOU PURSUE YOUR BUSINESS
Explain the process {ups and downs}

My father, Raymond Barney, who is an accomplished business owner says, "Some people like the security of making a check every couple of weeks. Then there are some people who don't mind putting in the effort and taking the chance to see whatever amount of money that will make them."

I love entrepreneurship! I came from a family of entrepreneurs. My grandfather was one of the first Black businessmen in Chicago to be a record wholesaler. This was a pretty big accomplishment in racist Chicago during the 60's and 70's. My father then got into the business, after college and continues to run our family-owned health food store. I saw my grandfather and father work hard to achieve their dreams for their family. My drive, my perseverance and motivation to create my business came from my family!

I started my business during a season of lack. I was at a company for five years and had not received a salary increase for four years. In this season I was complacent, depressed and stressed, but knew I had to create another stream of income. Coming to terms that I have always loved human resources, I took my existing skills and talent of what I practiced every day as a human resources practitioner and applied it to starting a business.

Some of the best businesses were started during a season of lack. This motivation consistently drives me and I will never forget how I got started.

3: TIPS FOR ELEVATING, SUCCESS, INSPIRATION, GROWTH + PUSHING THROUGH

My mother, Robye Scott who works in Diversity for a major company says, "Employee resource groups constantly bring in branding experts to support employees in building their careers. It is the belief that companies make this investment, because they believe that in order to make a significant impact on the bottom line, employees must first know who they are and what they stand for."

Tips to Help You Succeed with Presenting Your Brand Value:

- Know Your Value – Demand Your Worth!

Do not discount yourself or your service offerings. Your brand is sellable! You have done the work, you have gotten the education and you have the experience. Your brand is why people buy-in to you.

- Believe in your product/service brand!

If you do not believe in your product/service brand, who will? Do not short change your value and service offerings. People are buying into your experience, education and accomplishments.

- Be clear about your brand!

How far can you go if you are not clear about what you stand for – your brand? Stand firm and be clear about your mission/vision.

- How do people perceive you?

Ask your clients/customers, friends and family one question; what does my business brand say to you? Ask them to be totally honest, as this is important to your business growth and development.

- Hire Your Brand!

Would you hire your brand today? Be honest. Is your brand marketable? When people hire you what do they get? What are you selling them?

Be a business brand that people can trust and believe in! Be a brand that attracts potential applicants, especially if you're looking to grow, expand and hire future staff.

- Always Seek Professional Development!

Always attend classes, seminars, read business books, etc. You are an expert in your field and industry, always be aware of the trends.

- Practice Subjectivity and Objectivity Negotiation!

The subjectivity is having your customer buy-in to your charisma, your personality, your drive, your attitude and demeanor. In essence, this is you as a person.

Get the lesson and learn from it, don't let history repeat itself. We have all had to endure challenges with not being accepted, but in that you grow, you learn and you get better!

Your brand is your business and it is what you stand for! Learn from your business mistakes and grow.

Remember, all things work together for your good! Stay encouraged and keep the faith!

God Bless You on the Business Journey,

Rai

18

The Process of Success
Tonya Biglow

• • •

You were born to be successful. Everything within you serves to guide you towards a successful lifestyle. Not by force and not by maneuvering, but by the natural flow of the universe that says we are designed to be great. You are great – most people just don't know it yet. Moreover, most people who have achieved a certain level of success have not even begun to see the magnitude of magnificence they actually possess. Most people who have achieved success early on in life either fall into one of two categories. Either they were trained to succeed or they have the innate desire to achieve and just through sheer oblivion – believed that success was in their reach.

The truth is, both can continue to maintain their level of success. However, for the one without training, this chapter will serve as the source of you knowing exactly how you were able to obtain what you have thus far and how to grow faster than ever before.

Now, for those who have achieved much and lost more, you could be in a position of finding it very difficult to get it back. For you I say – hold on tight! For the ride you are about to embark upon will show you exactly where you fell off but more importantly how to get back on the ride and continue riding into the sunset.

Additionally, for those who so desperately desire more or those who have searched and tried repeatedly to succeed but to no avail, this chapter will be your strength. It will identify where you are as well as assist you in understanding that true success is closer than you think, with less effort I might add.

Rest assured – no matter if you are looking for more understating on how to become successful or just looking for more insight on the matter, this chapter will serve as a quick guide to help you achieve what you desire. Fast!

It's time to go get your success!

We will begin with some very clear definitions. Most of the information you will read will be what you may consider common sense. It will provide you with phrases and suggestions that will seem like it's not realistic or that more work should be involved. Most people look at success and believe that it is very difficult to obtain. I say on the contrary. Success and the action that's required to take you to the next level are somewhat easy. The only difficulty is that people are generally not willing to master the mundane and repetition until they reach the desired result. They tend to abandon the "easy" work and take on tasks that are more difficult in nature and therefore – in their mind's eye – must be the key to success.

Let's take what happens when you plant a seed. That seed will do nothing until placed in an environment conducive to growth. If you just keep the seed in your hand, it will remain a seed. If you place the seed on the table, it will remain a seed. However, when you place the seed into soil it has the potential to grow.

The soil becomes the right environment if it has been treated properly. The ground must be prepared to receive the seed. Once placed in good ground, nourishment must still take place in the form of sun and water to help provide the proper nutrients and chemicals needed for growth to occur. Once the right amount of nutrients are fed into the seed, the seed dies, the surface breaks and a small stem emerges through searching for a more direct connection with the "good stuff", I like to call it. This will further aid the growth of the seed. After a certain amount of time, you will begin to see a tremendous amount of action – I like to call it energy in the works. Moreover, you will soon see a full-grown flower, tree or whatever type of seed you have planted.

This is nature and resembles the "grow process". In order for people to grow, they need to go through this exact same process. For success is a process. It is strategic and the rules apply for every person who wants it.

Know Who You Are and What You Want

Now just like there are different gestational periods for various kinds of seed, there are different gestational periods for your levels of success. This unfortunately varies from person to person; there is no magic bullet to provide a specific time frame for any one person to achieve success. For it is truly at the mercy of the universe. Nevertheless, I can tell you this; the more energy (belief) you give your seed (success), the more sunlight (visibility) you provide it and the better prepared the ground is (preparation work) the faster your process of success will be as it flourishes into the beautiful flowers you have planted.

Believe You Deserve What You Want
Your self-identity will dictate how high or how low you go in life.

If you can picture it in your mind, believe it in your heart and feel it in your spirit – you will have it. Now the situation here is that it does not matter if the thought is good or not good; high or low vibration thoughts, thoughts of wealth or thoughts of poverty, thoughts of power or thoughts of inadequacies; whatever you "believe" know that it will happen.

Now it is right here where most people really get caught up. Most say to themselves. *But I don't want a bad marriage. I don't want this miserable job. I don't want to be broke*. Or whatever it is that you are complaining about right now. The truth of the matter is, if what you don't want is the only thing on your mind then that is what you will continue to get.

If your self-identity says only people who have a college degree can make a 6-figure salary, and you don't have a degree, guess what? Your self-identity will never allow you to accomplish your goal. I know a 6-figure salary is what you want but your self-identity does not line up with the definition that you have outlined. What you have is all you believe you can have at this time and unless you make some changes in your self-identity then what you have is what you will continue to have for the rest of your life. But if you want more there is something you can do about it!

Take Action
Most often, it takes more energy to begin the process than it does to complete the process. While studying Newton's law of motion while obtaining my physics degree, I learned that an object resting will remain at rest unless an external force acts upon it. Conversely, an object in motion will not change its velocity unless an external force acts upon it. In other words, you have to move in order to get moving. No one can make you do this. This part is up to you.

Take possession of your own mind. Free yourself from fears and doubts, from worries and woes, from lack and limitations. Move now, from a poverty mindset to a mindset of prosperity, from lack to loads of loot (money) filling your bank account. You can move from fear to freedom or from doubts to dreaming. It is possible to change from worrying to winning or from limitations to living life with no limits. If it was possible for others, it is just as possible for you.

As you read this chapter, you may or may not be ready to receive this data. From my years of mentoring and working on myself, I have learned the following, "Some will, some won't and some wait." Nevertheless, I do know this, the moment you receive this information, your life will immediately begin to change. Your actions will change; your direction will change and how you view yourself will change.

How Do I Change?
Well, there is a lot of information shared with us every day. Most of which we ignore or tune out, but there are some things that we have heard or through our experiences that we choose to lock into our belief system. Most people choose to limit what we can do to what we can get from outside of ourselves. The reality; you already have what it takes to create the success you want.

If you notice – the seeds of success has nothing to do with going to school, getting good grades and then getting a good job. Let me ask you this, how many wealthy employees do you know? Right – me either! The only way to become financially free is to create it. It does not matter how many times you may have failed in the past. It does not matter how much education you may have right now. What matters is how you see yourself. Look in the inner-mirror and tell yourself what you see.

We set our own limitations by focusing on what we cannot do. To totally turn your life around and go toward the direction you consciously want, you must see yourself as you want to be. It is only then that your actions will line up with your unconscious thoughts. Until then, you will continue seeing what you don't like.

Feel like you have no control? Try using your mind. Focusing solely on that which you want and learn just how much control you have. Not just having control over other things but over yourself. Your mind is the one thing that no one can control unless you give someone access to it. Now I must admit – it is easy to fall prey to the songs of this world. They are so harmonious and beautiful. They tend to call unto you like a light calls to the insect. And although the light is beautiful and draws the insect into its space – we all know what happens once the insect gets too close to the light – no more bug. There is no difference with you. If you allow the cares of the world and the propaganda from the media to engulf your mind then your outcome will be the same as the insect – utter destruction.

Stay clear of believing any news that will take away from that which you want. Do not believe that there is only one way to get what you want. I learned a long time ago, if you truly want to get ahead of the crowd – observe what everyone else is doing and then do the total opposite. That is how the good become great.

19

Anything is Possible!
Ocie Duncan IV

• • •

I know you're on this road like the rest of us, going past all the stops that teach us, edify us, and define who we really are in this world. We all deserve happiness, love, tears of joy, the very feeling of satisfaction from our life, and I this is my way of reminding you that anything is possible! If you're reading this book, then you're probably on the right path. I'd like to believe that I am one of those "Chosen 144,000 Few of God". I'm here to encourage you, enlighten you, as well as empower you on this path of success. You must note that your mindset plays a big role in your success, and your overall enjoyment of life. Also, I added some quotes at the end of the chapter. Remember that your thoughts, emotions, and desires help craft the manifestations your life.

I'm currently 22 years of age, I drive a Mercedes Benz, I'm very grateful for all the experience, and experiences my creator has given me. I am a part-owner of LotteryPick®/Urban Motive Inc. We have a healthy and delicious energy drink and sportswear line. The Energy drink is sold at Walgreens, and other retail locations, gas stations, liquor stores, etc. I've been in million dollar meetings, and have presented awards at award shows we sponsored. I stumbled across the opportunity with LotteryPick while doing cold calls for my marketing company. While looking through all of the business cards I had acquired overtime back then, I found a "funky" looking flyer with a can on it. I don't remember when or where I got it. But I made the call, gave my sales pitch, and I was given an opportunity to work LotteryPick Energy Drink's first Walgreen's taste sampling. After that, I was given the title of "External Affairs", and then years later, I was offered a contract to become part-owner of the company.

I've been blessed with many surreal opportunities in my life, some that people would pay millions to experience, and the some that may be a little too explicit. I genuinely and unconditionally love helping people; I feel like that was a calling of mine. There's something priceless, and empowering about positive change. Personally, I've been focused more on edifying myself every day, someway, somehow through self-mastery, working out, meditation, increasing brand awareness of LotteryPick, and making the world a better place.

I believe we are limited by our beliefs; we live in a universe of infinite possibilities, but sometimes limit them to one or two. Believe it or not, I was blessed to drive a $225,000 Bentley Continental GT V8, which is one of my many testimonies. Life is meant to be enjoyed, but is actually purposed for progress, so you can be built into something greater. Wouldn't you want a life of purpose?

Everyone likes to see growth in some manner, especially for themselves, and others. You deserve that growth in your life, those dreams to become a reality. I am here to show you that anything is possible!

I am also blessed to be a humanitarian award winning motivational speaker. I have spoken at many Chicago Public Schools, as well as charter schools. I remember back when I first thought about wanting to help the next generation of urban youth coming up, and now it's all a reality. I generally speak to youth about life issues such as alternatives to violence, career development, making good decisions, and following your dreams. I've even spoken at concerts with Diggy Simmons, and The OMG Girls headlining the show, and because of my acting on a popular tv show in Chicago "All About Chris" (2012-2013), I found myself getting used to taking pictures and signing autographs after my speaking in classrooms. Even in 2015 I still get noticed by fans throughout Chicago, and a few times outside of Chicago, but mostly whenever I am around the city.

In 2011, I could've walked five blocks down the street from my home, and see my face on a billboard. Not to mention the other billboard I was on by the expressway for Effortless Style Studio on 95th and Stony Island, in Chicago. All of these opportunities just came my way through putting forth effort in business with positive intention, tact, skill, understanding and technique. I will also add that my faith played a big role in my life; because everything went so perfectly, I couldn't have done all this alone.

In 2012, I had realized that I was doing everything I've ever wanted. I was acting on a popular local tv show, which led to me to acting in stage plays. One was actually backed by popular demand at the Harold Washington Cultural Center. I was also featured in an article for my acting in TrueStar Magazine. So, as the LotteryPick sales were going up, suddenly, everywhere I went someone noticed me from TV. This was so surreal, but I got used to it over time.

Near the end of 2013, I had accomplished all I really wanted, pertaining to my career.

•I am part owner of an energy drink/sportswear line.
•I received recognition for my accomplishments on a billboard near my home and a popular expressway.
• I was a chosen to receive an award at The 32nd Annual Chicago Music Awards.
• I obtained an acting role in a popular weekly TV show and I often found myself signing autographs for and taking pictures with fans of the show.
• Sometimes I'd just go outside and randomly get noticed by fans of the show, and surprisingly I still do!

My career life was, and is still rewarding, and exciting, but I realized I wanted more. I realized there was more to life than just material things and the world's vices. I've seen myself doing the impossible on numerous occasions, and I'm just thankful to be able to share such experiences.

Anything is possible!

Here's one of my favorites, the Bentley Story.

Bentley- I'll never forget the day I drove a 2012 Bentley Continental GT V8 in downtown Chicago, on Lake Shore Drive. I was in the car with a new business partner of mine, and we were dropping off my ex-wife to the Red Line train. Surprisingly, I was looking at a Bentley in a magazine at Wal-mart same day, same place, when I met this guy. This is back when I was married to whom I thought was my dream girl, but it wasn't working out. So he says as we're getting on the Dan Ryan expressway, "We gonna get you in a Bentley today." I nodded with a bit of skepticism, saying to myself, *that's bullshit*. But it actually happened. The moment we parked, my new partner says, "Remember to ask for the bill of sale." I acknowledged him as we walked into the dealership.

A gentleman walked up to us as we entered the dealership, and shook our hands. He asked me, "What are you interested in checking out?" I said, "The Bentley Continental GT." He shows me a blue one on his phone, and says, "It's $20,000 down, if you want to order the car. Also what do you do professionally?" I said that I was an actor on a popular TV show with the (should this be 'geared to?' urban youth (which was true) I don't think 'which was true' is necessary. So we walked over to the v12, I'm in the driver's seat, and an expert comes out to tell me about the car. After giving me thorough detail of the car's performance, he says "We don't have the v12 outside, would you like to try out the v8?" I replied calmly with a nonchalant demeanor, "Uhh sure, why not." I

199

could never forget that day. I drove a $225,000 car, and it was amazing! You could switch the suspension from comfort to sport and there was a special gear for more power. I felt like I was once again being rewarded for being fearless. But I was grateful and in awe, if anything. God is good.

Here are some quotes that represent my philosophy on life and business, hope you enjoy.

Quotes

"Everyone deserves to be happy not just you."

"Life is a beautiful thing, I hope you appreciate it."

"Karma is there to help you learn, as well as to push you forward in life."

"Silence is sometimes the best answer."

"You deserve everything you want, but you must believe it first!"

"By your standards you are imperfect, but by God's

I want to thank the ones who helped me on this path of greatness.

20

First Things First
Tiffany M. Stevens

• • •

As an entrepreneur, you will be faced with many challenges. Some of your challenges will be internal, such as self-doubt, fear, a lack of faith, and procrastination. Sometimes, you might question if you are in the right business, or should even be in business at all. External challenges can be viewed as; competition, negative people, rejection, inability to attract customers, and financial issues. These challenges could ultimately leave you feeling stressed out and unequipped to manage your business affairs. Like challenges, storms are going to come. So, it's necessary to build a solid foundation that can withstand the storm. When the foundation is strong, you can stand tall and be who you were created to be regardless of the circumstance.

Having a strong foundation is crucial; not only pertaining to success, but for your overall well-being. By putting first things first, you will quickly realize that you have the power to change your thoughts, beliefs, and actions.

Once those three are changed, self-doubt, fear, procrastination, and any other negative thought or feeling that has been holding you back will dissipate. Just as you have the power to manage your internal challenges, you will also realize that it is solely up to you to choose your reactions to the external challenges.

When you are prepared and equipped with faith in a higher power, facing life's challenges won't be as difficult or scary. The challenges won't impact you the same. You will begin to view problems as learning opportunities. When you choose to put your mind in alignment with the will of your higher power, you will be connected to the omniscience of the universe and can fulfill your purpose with confidence. Simply put, life works better when you put first things first. When your life works, chances are your business will too. You may find it difficult or nearly impossible to have a thriving and profitable business when your personal life seems out of order.

There are four principles that I follow to ensure that I am always putting first things first. These principles provide me with guidelines to determine my priorities, to fulfill my purpose, and to follow my path toward success. My four principles are: **Believe In and Have Faith in a Higher Power, Live on Purpose; Have a Dream Team; and to Have Personal Integrity and Value Time.** In this chapter, I will share the principles that influence my process as an entrepreneur. I invite you to also put into practice the four basic principles that has helped me put and keep first things first.

Believe In and Have Faith in a Higher Power

Three ways to strengthen your faith and connect to your higher power is through prayer, meditation and practice. Prayer is a consciousness raising tool. What you have in your personal life and business is a direct result of your consciousness. In other words, watch your thoughts and beliefs! Everything that you experience in life is largely influenced by what you believe. To begin building, or to maintain a consciousness of success and prosperity, you must schedule time to commune with your higher power through prayer and meditation. During the quiet time that you set aside, you are intentionally engaging in an activity that prepares and trains your mind to become aware of all the good that is around and available to you. Mediation may mean many things for many people, depending on who you ask. In this context, I would like to define meditation as a state of consciousness entered into for the purpose of putting one in touch with Divine Mind so that the soul may listen to the voice of one's higher power. It's not only a way to relax the mind and body, but can also be used to connect us to the spiritual resources that we all have. Meditation is another form of prayer, and is also known as the listening or the way that we receive thoughts, ideas, and instructions. After connecting to your higher power through prayer and meditation, it's time to be obedient and put all that you have received into practice.

Live on Purpose

Keep the main thing...the main thing! My purpose is to give love and motivation to women and girls that have been impacted by sexual and domestic violence. I help facilitate their healing and I am there with them on their healing journey. In my organization, The Glam Foundation as well as in the work that I do, every goal and action is influenced by and is in alignment with my purpose. I have found that when I am doing what I love to do, what's important to me and what I am good at, the right people, opportunities and resources seems to present themselves. If you do not already have a Purpose Statement, I strongly encourage you to create one. Once you become aware of your purpose, everything that you do can be planned and geared towards fulfilling that purpose.

When creating your Purpose Statement, be mindful of WHY it is that you want to do...what you want to do. Intentions are important to consider because the unseen reason for doing anything is in the intention. Believe it or not, it's actually the intention of an act, not the act itself that sets the Universal Law of cause and effect into motion.

Whenever I am asked to do something, or to partner with another organization, one of the first questions that I ask myself is, how does it support my purpose and mission? If it does not support the purpose and mission, why do it? Now, this doesn't mean that I won't do it but asking these questions allows me to be clear about what my intentions are. When I was invited to contribute to the book that you are now reading, The Entrepreneur Within, I spent most of the time praying for direction on what to write about and for clarification on why.

I wanted to be true to myself and to my purpose while offering you, the reader practical and useful information. When you understand why you are here and what you were created to do, you are more likely to stay on the path to success. Living on purpose is also being aware of the people and things that you have in your life that don't support your purpose, growth, or development. Years ago, I used to laugh at myself for choosing a profession in which I had to continuously read, study, and attend trainings and workshops. Now, I fully understand the benefits and feel that anyone that considers themselves an expert in a particular area or field must be committed to lifelong learning and self-improvement.

In addition to reading books, and attending trainings and conferences, I suggest investing in a QUALIFIED Coach and joining or forming a mastermind group. A good coach will assist you with clarifying your purpose, goals, and visions while supporting you through the internal and external challenges that will appear. Be very selective when choosing a coach and don't be afraid to make the investment. Mastermind groups allow you to meet with other like-minded individuals to network, brainstorm, problem-solve, and provide motivation and encouragement. Mastermind partners hold one another accountable, which could be the key to getting on or staying on the path to success.

Have a Dream Team
For many years, I felt that I didn't need a team and that I could do it on my own. I was wrong! Getting the right people on the team is essential. Building a team is not

easy and takes work, patience, and discernment. The first step to building a great team is making sure that the right people are on the team. The right people are going to be hard working. They are going to believe in and see the vision of the business and want to work hard to support the mission. When you have trustworthy, resourceful and talented people on your team, it's important to have them in the right position on the team. Allowing people to bring more of themselves and their talents into the position will boost their purpose. When connecting personal purpose to the organization's purpose, everybody wins. It goes without saying that at times you will have to clean house.

If there are people on the team that are lazy time wasters with negative energy...LET THEM GO. Getting the wrong people off the team is in the best interest of everyone involved and for the overall success of the business.

Have Personal Integrity and Value Time
Integrity is defined as the quality of being honest and having strong moral principle, or the state of being whole and undivided. Having personal integrity is being honest with yourself and being true to who you are. This practice did not come easy for me. I am passionate about advocating and raising awareness for Sexual and Domestic Violence. Yet, I know that it's not an easy topic to talk about because many people would rather avoid the topic all together. It was hard for me, so I decided that I wouldn't talk about it either. After all, I didn't want to make people feel uncomfortable. It was during one of my quiet moments in prayer and

meditation that I realized I was not being true to myself, to my passion, and in a sense to the population that I served. Now, everywhere I go, I talk about it! I am no longer afraid to speak out on violence against women. I now recognize that the more I talk about it, the less taboo it becomes and it helps more people find the courage to speak up and speak out.

Think about where you lack integrity in your personal life or in your business. Be honest about what's working and what's not working. Once you have the information, don't beat yourself up about what's not working. Use that data to inform you of possible growth opportunities. If you are not good at following up and handling administrative tasks, get an assistant. Virtual assistants are great for those that are just starting out or for those that has a small budget. If public speaking isn't your thing, join a Toastmaster's group. Be honest with yourself and whatever it is, devise a plan to clear it up.

Being in integrity is not always easy. In our culture, most people seem to be more interested in getting what they want...when they want it, no matter the cost. However, when you have faith in a higher power, you trust that higher power to be your source and know that everything will work for your good. That awareness gives you a sense of peace and comfort. Peace and comfort to know that you never have to allow circumstances to change your ethics. Maintaining your integrity may not be easy, but it's worth it.

Operating with integrity as it pertains to your time is huge. I hear many entrepreneurs complaining about time and feelings as if there are no days off. If that is the case for you, re-evaluating how you spend your time may be advantageous. True success is mastered when there is balance in the seven major areas of your life. I thought that I could conquer the world, end violence against women and watch 20 hours of TV per week. I was completely out of balance. I soon realized that I had to choose my purpose or my secret obsession with reality TV. I chose my purpose! Even after choosing my purpose, I still had to work through procrastination, the number one stealer of time and money.

Be honest with yourself, are you a procrastinator? Have you been spending time in other areas doing other things that could have been spent fulfilling your purpose?

Being an entrepreneur isn't easy and it takes courage, diligence and patience. It is my hope and prayer that the four practices shared in this chapter will help you along your journey to success. When you put first things first by building a strong foundation, you can overcome any challenge. Always live on purpose because it's the purpose that informs you and keep you on track. Build a team, be in integrity and enjoy the freedom and benefits of entrepreneurship. Always remember that.... the power to be and to do is in YOU!

21

Why What I Do Matters...
C. Lynn Williams
Ms. Parent Guru

• • •

I never really understood what my mother went through with me as a strong-willed daughter until I had my own children. After the childhood I had, I never wanted kids of my own. Kids were worrisome, needy and a pain in the neck! And they were yours forever! No, I didn't want children of my own. However after 3 or 4 years into my first marriage, I knew I wanted somebody that looked like me. Does that sound selfish? Yes I'll admit it was probably selfish, along with my parents and my in-laws asking constantly – **"WHEN WILL YOU HAVE KIDS?"**

My parenting journey began right here. From the beginning I believed that children were little adults with opinions and thoughts of their own. As idealistic as that sounds, once I decided to have children, I wanted to give them an opportunity to speak openly and honestly. My parenting ideas were not well-received by my mom and her side of the family, because she was raised to believe that children were seen and not heard. An outspoken kid was considered a disrespectful one. That was okay for her; I was more concerned with raising leaders and critical thinkers, not followers.

While my parenting journey began in the middle '80s, my career as a writer began a decade later. To be an impactful non-fiction writer, you have to have experiences to share with your audience. A painful divorce and family relocation left me with co-parenting responsibilities as well as the challenge of parenting with adults who had entirely different philosophies of what being a parent meant. That kind of life experience gave me a lot to think about, but more importantly solutions to share with other parents who would ultimately find their life in tatters and their families torn apart. Yes there is relief out here!

What I discovered during my times of brokenness, broken family and hormonal teenage years, was that God was still my source of strength. I discovered that patience and a guard over my tongue worked wonders for my relationship with my daughter. I learned that I had to hold my son accountable or he wouldn't grow to be a 'proper' man. I also realized that people would pay to hear my story.

I wasn't prepared for the rigors of writing when I began my first book. Sometimes, the words came quickly, and sometimes they didn't. I would work on my manuscript and believe I was done, and then realize that I hadn't ended it properly. Ugh... Then I would write more of my thoughts until the first book was completed.

While completing my first book was a great accomplishment, the hardest work had just begun! Having completed four books now, I realize there is a formula to writing a book. Start with any outline! Give yourself a goal such as, *I will write every day for one hour*. No distractions. Be prepared to credit and site your source if you use a quote from another author. I don't know about you, but I don't always see my errors until I print out my work. It's hard to catch them on the computer. Once I've read my work, I give it to someone else to proofread. I encourage you to do the same. Hire a professional proofreader or copy editor to read it. To me, there is nothing worse than seeing punctuation and spelling errors in someone's book. It's quite a turnoff!

Just like any other writer, I believed that my book would become an overnight success - a bestseller! When that didn't happen, I believed it was my publisher's responsibility to do everything possible to sell my book. Hey, let me be the one that informs you, that is **not** the norm. What I know is that you have to market yourself while you market your book! There are very few overnight successes.

When you write about topics that are difficult for the audience to accept or possibly understand, it's a good idea to have a very catchy (if not humorous) title and eye catching book cover. I never expected that my passion would be to write about how to be phenomenal parents! Children are generally as sacred as they come when you talk to a parent. But as I continued to raise my kids into adulthood, parenting became one of my passions, because I felt there was room for us to become better parents. A book about being a parent, didn't necessarily make it a subject that people wanted to run out, buy and read. What it meant was that I had to create the desire to read my books by starting a blog and talking about parenting topics, become a thought leader on social media sites like LinkedIn, create followers and follow others on Twitter, Instagram and Facebook. Is it necessary? Absolutely! People who are interested in your story need to know you exist.

7 Thoughts to Consider As You Begin to Write

Don't Quit – I cannot tell you how many times I decided that writing was NOT for me and I was going to find something more lucrative to do with my life. As the lady in the E-surance commercial says "That's not how it works." If you wake up and have been inspired to write a book, that's your calling at that wonderful moment. If you think about it, everyone has a story inside of them. The question is whether they intend to let the story out and inspire someone else, or leave it buried to be discovered in another lifetime.

Stay Encouraged – It is easy to allow people and circumstances to get you down. Maybe you are sending out your manuscript to publishers and keep receiving rejections. Or maybe you let one of your family members read your first chapter and they admit that they hate it! Jeez, I hope that doesn't happen, but if it does, find a way to stay encouraged. Read inspirational material or read the autobiography of famous authors and see what kinds of adversities they had to overcome in order to become successful.

Join an Authors' Group – I joined a couple of online organizations that are devoted to offering resources and advice for authors and bloggers. One of them is entitled **Where Writers Win**. It's chocked full of additional websites, fairs, book clubs that favor authors. In a word...this group is awesome and quite supportive! The other organization I joined is **World Literary Café** is an organization I joined as well. I love how this group support authors in addition to encouraging that support among authors on social media. You are given opportunities to promote your books for a very small fee. It's so beneficial seeing that it's a large network. If you need writing or editing support, they offer that as well. Here's the secret... both of those organizations are FREE to join!

Develop a Thick Skin – I probably said this in one of my earlier paragraphs, but it is so important that I'll say it again – "Develop a thick skin." By that I simply mean, try not to be offended if someone doesn't like what you wrote or how you wrote it, especially when you ask for a critique of your work. I agree it doesn't feel very good for someone to say – "You might want to rewrite this section...I don't understand what you mean." Those comments are designed to help you become a better writer. So accept them graciously and don't take it personally!

Write Consistently – As I write this, I laugh inside because this is precisely what I did not do when I wrote my first book, *Trying to Stay Sane While Raising Your Teen*. I was a very inexperienced writer and each time I sat down to write, it was usually at the end of another school year. Suffice to say, it took me about five years to write my first book! I took a class after that experience, and learned how to write a book in 90 days! It actually works if you follow the advice I offered at the beginning.

Continue to Read Works by Other Authors – When do I have time to read books by other authors, when I am writing my own books? Great question, but just do it. Consider it homework, especially if you are new to writing. It is a great way to measure your work with other authors; and you also get to see the style of how other authors writes.

Sharpen Your Saw – This is a term I learned in corporate America and it simply means, continue to take classes, read books, watch videos and/or hire a coach to help you get to the next level of your career as a writer. After completing my fourth book, I am a much better writer than I was when I started. Since your book is considered a 'calling card', what you learn may be the stepping stones needed to add speaking or coaching to your writing toolkit. I have met authors who proofread or publish other authors' works. Whether you pursue other avenues in addition to writing, sharpening your saw will be something you definitely want to do.

TEW JOURNAL

By Diane Brown

1. What would be the number one reason you would start a business? Is it an obsession or something you love?

2. When tough times arise, how will you react when faced with adversity?

3. Do you know your core competencies and how do you utilize them in your business?

4. What opportunities do you create for yourselves to develop solid connections to support your endeavor?

5. Do you have the tenacity, confidence and passion to push past "dream killers"?

6. How do you keep control of your time? Have you learned to say NO...unless you say no, you will never be in charge of your agenda.

7. How much of your free time do you give to help other entrepreneurs to help them with their strategic plan? Is that a wise utilization of your time?

8. Do you have a strategic plan for your business? Without a plan, you are setting yourself up to fail.

9. What do you do every day to build your personal brand?

10. How are your online marketing skills? What methods do you utilize to feel your brand and do you have a formula of the best times to post your information?

ACKNOWLEDGEMENTS

We would like to collectively thank our family, friends, spouses, children and all of those who have supported our journeys over the years. Without you, we would not be where we are today. We are grateful for opportunities of the past, present and future!

The Entrepreneur Within You

EMPOWERING, EQUIPPING, INSPIRING.
ENTREPRENEURS TO UNLEASH THEIR FULL POTENTIAL
WWW.TEWYOU.COM

Let's connect!
www.tewyou.com
www.twitter.com/tewyou

ABOUT THE AUTHOR

JULIE M. HOLLOWAY, THE CURATOR OF T.E.W.

 Julie M. Holloway is a multi-passion entrepreneur based in Chicago, Illinois. Her love for the arts began at the early age of eight. After high school, she attended Ringling School of Art & Design, DePaul and The Art Institute of Chicago where she took a variety of art courses and is currently pursuing her BA in Business Administration with a Marketing Focus at Capella University.

The first sixteen years of her career Holloway worked in various roles at companies such as Accenture, Home Depot, Nike and Oce Printing only to realize her passion and potential has and always will lie in the creative industry. After three years of moonlighting as an intrapreneur, while working a 12-14 hour workday, Holloway was spending 2-4 hours per night on her graphic design business. One day she woke up, realized it was her time to pursue her passion as a creative entrepreneur, took the ultimate leap of faith, and left her full-time career in corporate America.

Holloway opened JMH Cre8ive Solutions in November 2011 and has experienced tremendous growth and an expansion of creative design, print and web services along with her team of co-entrepreneurs. With an enormous heart and hunger for collaborating and assisting entrepreneurs carry through their creative vision, the business continues to flourish. Not too long ago, a colleague labeled JMH as the "dream midwife" because she has helped, encouraged, counseled and mentored many clients and colleagues as they pursue their entrepreneurial dreams.

In her spare time, JMH spends quality and creative time with her husband Darnell, children Jasmine (13) and D.J. (8) who are also emerging entrepreneurs. Together, the family loves sports, games, the Chicago White Sox, playing mini-golf and going to various events together. The kids are learning a bit about entrepreneurship by authoring books, selling soy wax candles, t-shirts, journals and more!

www.jmhcre8ive.com
www.juliemholloway.com
www.facebook.com/jmhcreativesolutions
www.tewyou.com
www.twitter.com/tewyou
www.facebook.com/theentrepreneurwithinyou